# A NOBLE QUEEN

# A NOBLE QUEEN

## A Romance of Indian History

MEADOWS TAYLOR

*'O, never was there queen*
*So mightily betray'd!*
*—Antony and Cleopatra*
*act i. sc. iii.*

GYAN

*Published by*

Gyan Publishing House
5, Ansari Road
Daryaganj, New Delhi-110002
Phone: 011-47034999, 9811692060
E-mail: books@gyanbooks.com

*Distribution Network*
gyanbooks.com
India, USA, Canada, UK, Australia, France



ISBN : 978-81-212-3825-0 (PB)
First Published, 1896

2nd Impression 2020

*Printed at:* Gyan Press, Delhi.



**A Noble Queen**
Author: Meadows Taylor

# CONTENTS

OF

# THE THIRD VOLUME.

## *BOOK IV.*



## *BOOK V.*

# A NOBLE QUEEN.

## BOOK IV.

### CHAPTER I.

#### THE KING'S ENTRY.

THE triumphal entry of King Ibrahim II. into his capital was not only a glorious sight to its people, but an assurance that the long and disastrous wars between the rival States of Beejapoor and Ahmednugger were at an end. King Ibrahim had kept the field against the conspiracy of his cousin, the Prince Ismail, who was supported by a large portion of his own army under Eyn-ool-Moolk, and by his uncle, Boorhan Nizam, Shah of Ahmednugger; and against the possible advance of the Portuguese of Goa, whose skill in war was well known in the Dekhan. The King of Ahmednugger, however, could make no impression on the Beejapoor troops, who defended the frontier stoutly, and, falling ill, died in his camp at Puraindah. His son Ibrahim, a youth, was placed upon the throne, and soon after again pressed the war against Beejapoor, which brought on the general action in which Humeed Khan, the uncle of Abbas Khan, had proved victorious; and as the troops of Ahmednugger fled from the field with the loss of the whole of their artillery and war elephants, the long continued struggle came to an end, and the Royal army returned to Beejapoor, escorting their King in triumph. "On the 18th Mohorrum," writes the historian of the period, "the King made a triumphant entry into Beejapoor amid the acclamation of the people, who on this occasion had adorned the streets with gold and silver tissues, velvets, brocades, and other rich cloths and ornaments." But it was not the splendour of the spectacle which gratified the people; it was the assurance of safety and security from further disturbance, for which all were thankful. Those who had wavered in their allegiance now declared a hearty loyalty; and the southern invaders, under the Hindoo Prince of Penkonda, who had joined the conspiracy on the assurance of the conspirators that they might thus regain the dominions they had lost, having been defeated and driven back, there remained no part of the Beejapoor dominions that was not in profound peace after a long series of years of rebellion; and the people rejoiced in a real gladness which had not been felt for several generations.

As we already know, the force under Abbas Khan had marched

northwards to the aid of the King; but as the rainy season was at its height, King Ibrahim had taken up his position at the fort of Shahdroog, or Nuldroog, and had left Humeed Khan with the main body of the army to watch the frontier and repel incursion should it take place. Abbas Khan, therefore, on receiving orders from the King, had marched to join his uncle, and arrived in time to take part in the finally victorious battle.

From his uncle he had received a very hearty and affectionate welcome, the particulars of which need not be recorded here; and it was with a great satisfaction that the veteran commander heard the details of the combat in the presence of the Queen Dowager, and the discovery of Osman Beg's treason. Abbas Khan had, indeed, to recount all the passages in his life which we already know of, which to his uncle had been so grievously misrepresented. There was nothing left but for Abbas Khan to show his valour in the next engagement that ensued, which proved to be a very severe one, for the left wing of the Beejapoor troops was broken by an impetuous charge of ten thousand of the Ahmednugger cavalry. Many nobles and high officers of rank were slain, and many fugitives rode at once to the King's camp declaring that the whole army had been routed. For three days the King was in the last degree of anxious uncertainty, till a despatch from Humeed Khan, sent by the hand of his nephew, who could describe the action, assured him of the most perfect victory. Then it was, too, that the day might have gone hard for the Royal army but for the exertions and daring bravery of the fresh force under his nephew; and he related, also, how bravely the enemy's heavy battery had been stormed by the Beydurs, who appeared unconscious of danger, and how both Abyssinians and Dekhan cavalry had vied with each other under their young leader. In a few days the King's forces joined those under Humeed Khan near Sholapoor, where public thanksgiving was made for the close of the war, and some rewards and honours were publicly bestowed. But the grand ceremony of all was to take place at Beejapoor on the day of entry into the capital; and the King, carrying with him the whole of his army, with the trophies in artillery and elephants, Royal camp equipage and treasure that had been won, crossed the Bheema river slowly, and, as we know, safely reached his destination.

While in camp together, our friends Runga Naik and Abbas Khan had held many an anxious conversation on the subject of the old Syud Dervish and Zóra. Runga had told him of the forcible abduction of the girl, and of her rescue by himself and Burma; how, when he was obliged to leave Korikul, he had made her and the Syud over to Burma's care, but from that time he had no news of them.

If they had left Kukeyra they might be at Sugger, or, possibly, had gone on to Gulburgah; but nothing could be known for certain till the men who were returning from his own force should reach their territory, and either bring the old man and Zóra with them to camp or to Beejapoor. It was this very party which, crossing the country direct from the Royal camp, so providentially rescued Zóra, unharmed, and took her to her grandfather; and regulating their movements by those of the King himself, arrived in time to witness his triumphal entry. I trust this slight digression will be pardoned, for, indeed, without it the position of the parties would hardly be understood with exactness.

After the slight interruption caused by raising the infirm old man, the grand march was resumed; and the young King rode on, with the bitter cry of the old Syud, "Daad! Daad! Justice! Justice!" ringing in his ears, and the sightless eyes and feeble arms raised to heaven. Abbas Khan's tale had distressed him seriously; but he was here face to face with one instance of the first King Ibrahim's cruelty, and the sin of it rested on his house. Well, it could be condoned, perhaps, for the curse of a holy Syud could hardly be averted even by penance; but he would do, as he had vowed to Alla, what it was possible to do ere the sun set. So the young Monarch rode on in his pride; Humeed Khan on his right hand, Soheil Khan and the brave commander on his left, preceded by his gold and silver mace-bearers shouting his titles, and followed by the crowds of nobles and officers who composed his train. The day was as yet young, but it was bright and clear; and the flood of light glittering on morion and coat of mail, on cuirass and greave, on trappings and housings of gold and silver cloth, on banners and standards, and the great white buildings and palaces which stood out against the clear, deep blue sky, formed a combination of splendour which the mind can hardly realise, and which was well-nigh overpowering to all who saw it.

As to Zóra, she—who had seen nothing in all her life of splendour such as that—was fairly overpowered. She trembled, and her cheeks flushed as the first portion of the troops issued from the gate and passed them, drowning the feeble chaunt she and her grandfather were raising. But alms were showered upon them, and Ahmed had gathered up several times already what lay on the sheet. When the hoarse cry arose of "The King cometh! The King cometh!" and all heads bowed to the earth as he passed on, she did not think of him, but of one that might be with him. And yet, if he were, would he remember her? Would he even see her? Ah! it was an anxious moment, and her beating heart fluttered till she could hardly breathe. As the glorious pageant went slowly past, she could see the face she sought distinctly. Abbas Khan was riding near his uncle, conversing joyously with him and others around him; and the appearance of the gallant cavalier, dressed in glittering armour and cloth of gold, was almost too dazzling to look at. There were hundreds of Fakeers lining the road, crying for alms in stentorian voices. How would the faint chaunt of an infirm old man and a girl be heard amidst the din—the jangling bells of elephants, the neighing of excited horses, and the cries of the Royal titles? And Abbas Khan must have passed the group but for the sudden action of her grandfather, who threw himself forward with his shrill cry. Even then the grooms who ran by the King's horse, which had been somewhat startled, would have removed the old man, roughly enough, perhaps, from the Royal path; but the action of Abbas Khan had been rapid, and instantaneous, and decisive. What he had said to the King she could not hear; but the King's reply, "Bring him to the palace instantly," at once gave her the assurance she needed. Now Abbas Khan had dismounted, and stood embracing her grandfather; and was telling Runga Naik, who had seen all, to seek for his litter, which was under some trees at a little distance. Poor Zóra had not been able to obtain one at Almella, and she had ridden her own stout pony, which was also brought up; and she was preparing to mount it when Abbas Khan cried, "Stay, Zóra! not in this crowd; here is a palanquin of the King's for thee." So she entered it, shut the doors, and was carried on. There was no time for words. The whole scene was to her so altogether strange and unexpected that she could not find speech to thank any one; and as she shut the doors of the palanquin, and was safe from observation, her over-charged heart found relief in a burst of grateful sobs and tears.

As the King's procession went on towards the city, outside the walls, for he had to receive the blessing of the Chishtee priest whom we know of, it was easy for Abbas Khan to turn off with his charge into the gate of the citadel, while Runga Naik brought up the baggage ponies behind. All was comparatively clear in the citadel, and would be till the King arrived; so that Abbas Khan had no difficulty in speaking to one of the chief eunuchs of the private apartments, whom he knew, and putting his old friend and Zóra under his charge. He could not stay; and galloping after the procession soon overtook it, and resumed his place by his uncle's side.

"Who was the girl beside the old man who helped to raise him up, and whom my horse well nigh trampled down? I never saw a more beautiful and expressive face in my life," said his uncle with, as it seemed, a peculiar smile.

"She is the old saint's granddaughter, sir; and has devoted her life to him. Yes, she is beautiful."

"Then thou hast seen her, Abbas?"

"I have, uncle. The night I was in delirium at Juldroog she watched me, and gave me medicine and cool sherbet; but I could only see her face as that of one in a dream, and I have never looked on it since but once, and that only as a passing glance, till to-day, when I could not help seeing her, for the handkerchief she had tied over her turban had fallen off. It is evident that the

Syud hath taken the vow, perhaps at Gulburgah, where His Highness Geesoo Duráz made him a Wallee."

"Was he a Fakeer before then?" asked his uncle.

"No, sir. Though he called himself a Dervish, yet he had not taken any degree as a Fakeer, and people only called him Dervish. When he confided to me his identity his chief prayer was to be allowed to go free, that he might pay his vows at Sugger and Gulburgah, where, it appears, he was raised at once to the highest rank; and his title now is Luteef Shah Wallee. His is a sad story, uncle. Dost thou remember it?"

"I was a mere boy then," was the reply, "and used to attend the durbar with thy grandfather; but I quite remember the sadness with which all the city heard that Syud Ahmed Ali, the physician, had been blinded and sent to Juldroog. Everyone grieved for him, for he was not only the most learned of all at Court, but the most charitable. Many will remember him, and Ekhlas Khan was an intimate friend. Yea, it will cause a murmur in durbar when his name is mentioned, for he has been clean forgotten; and it was believed he had died soon after he was imprisoned. And thou hast told the King all?"

"All," replied the young Khan. "As the old Dervish told the tale to me, so did I repeat it faithfully; and I told him, too, how, under the Lord's will, he had saved my life."

"And what said he?"

"He wept, uncle; and said that the curse of a Syud should never rest upon the Adil Shah's realm or people; that search should be made for the Dervish. Then one day there came a holy man with a great retinue from Gulburgah, and told him—I was there—how a Fakeer had preached in the mosque, and a miracle had been done, and the heretofore Dervish had been made a Wallee at once, as the people demanded. And the King said to me, 'Thou art witness, Abbas Khan, that if I ever am blessed by the old man I will restore to him and his all he has lost.'"

"And he will do it, too," replied Humeed Khan. "And amidst the rejoicings of to-day one heart will be gladdened."

"Ameen! Ameen!" was the reply; and the conversation dropped.

## CHAPTER II.

### PARDON.

MEANWHILE Zóra and her grandfather had been conducted by the eunuchs through the entrance corridor into a suite of small but elegant apartments, which opened into a court and garden behind the palace. Their servants were brought in by a separate passage into a little kitchen and adjoining room; and there were baths and everything necessary for a pleasant, though necessarily confined residence. Here Zóra and old Mamoolla soon spread her grandfather's carpets, and they found cushions and bedsteads already provided. Presently, when all was arranged, Zóra led the old man to the cushions, and he sat down with a sigh of thankfulness.

"Where am I?" he said. "Surely I heard Meeah's voice? Where has he gone? Bring him to me."

"You are in the King's palace," said Zóra, throwing her arms around him. "Be thankful, Abba, that all thy sorrows and trials are over. We are safe in our refuge at last."

"Yes," he said, "at last! More than forty years have passed

over me since they sent me away to exile, blinded and in torment. Dost thou think I have forgotten that?"

"O, Abba!" cried the girl, putting her hand over his mouth, "didst thou not tell me when the Fateha was said before the tomb at Gogi that thou hadst forgiven King Ibrahim? Was it for thy blindness, Abba?"

"I am again rebuked, Zóra, and will forgive still; but it is hard to forget the past, and the joy with which I came forth from Almella, and within an hour was taken out, blind and bleeding! Forgive me, child! that I am false to thee. And forgive me, O Ibrahim! who hast received me back, that this bitter thought should have come into my mind. Yes, as I entered, I felt I was within the palace. This I am sure, by the turns we took as we entered, was the very apartment which I used to dwell in whenever my visit was prolonged. I even now scent the jessamine and tube roses of the little garden, and I feel as though I were in my old seat, with the soft south wind blowing on me. Methinks I see the blue Damascus tiles which are inlaid round the arches, and the carved window of the Zenana beyond."

"It is even so, Abba," said Zóra, much moved, as her grandfather pointed out the several objects with his finger. "Nothing has been changed; everything is as perfect now as it was then, and looks as quiet and peaceful as our little Zenana used to do at Juldroog."

"But it is only a gilded cage, my child; and I shall long to be free again, and to teach and preach, ay, and beg as I used to do even at Juldroog. And here there is more to do, else the Lord had not brought me."

"But, Abba, dear Abba!" began Zóra; and he interrupted her with, "Be patient, child! Dost thou think I do not welcome this as a place of rest, even as thou dost? And when Meeah comes he may bestow us elsewhere, when we can go and come with freedom. Then we shall have our own house, and our own servants, and palanquin, and bearers; and a sweet garden where I shall love to sit and discourse on the mysteries of holiness with the learned of the city, and on medicine with the physicians; and thou wilt have thy pigeons and flowers, and find out poor people and relieve them."

"Enough, enough, Abba!" cried Zóra, laughing and crying at the same moment. "Thou wouldst make a princess of me at once, and art tempting me by a hundred delightful anticipations fit but for the noble and great. But I see only my Fakeer's garments, and think of my uncompleted vows. And after all, am I not your humble little Zóra?"

"Thou art my precious treasure, child!" replied the old man, with emotion; "and the most noble house in Dekhan cannot produce one like thee."

Almost as he spoke, the curtain, which was drawn across the

entrance, was partly raised, and a man's voice said hurriedly to a companion, "The rooms are occupied by strangers, Maria; we must retire."

Zóra started to her feet, and rushed hastily forward. She saw two figures she at once recognised retreating into the corridor, and cried, "Maria! Maria! it is only your little Zóra; and Abba is here. Oh, come to us, we are alone."

In their turn Maria and her brother started. There was no doubt left when they saw the slight figure stretching out its arms with a low cry of joy, and the soft, flushed cheeks wet with tears; and a moment after they were locked in each other's arms, and approached the old man's seat, who was crying out joyfully, "Come! come to me, my friends; we are, indeed, with you at last. O Padré Sahib, thank the Lord with me that we are here safely, and in honour, for of a truth we have endured much."

Maria was not changed, save that the bright rosy colour of her cheeks had increased under the effects of better health; and she had attained a true majesty of beauty which far exceeded that which Zóra used to look on with wonder at Juldroog. Zóra seated her beside her on the cushions, but she could not give vent to her feelings of delight. Her loving brown eyes looked up like those of a dog to her friend; she threw her arms round her, and kissed her forehead, her eyes, her lips, passionately, hardly able to speak, except to say, "Thou art here, Maria, and restored to me.

Oh, yes, to me, who in all my troubles and tears have never forgotten thee; and this which thou gavest me," and she drew the little silver cross from her bosom, "has never left me, and has been my charm and deliverer of my honour when all hope of my deliverance seemed gone. And thou hast been happy, Maria?"

"Very happy, my darling," returned her friend, "longing to hear of you and Abba, but could obtain no news of you. Your little letter and the feather reached me safely, and I have them still at home. And I wrote a reply to you, Zóra, and my brother gave it to Abbas Khan, for I was able to write that the Queen had ordered Abba and you to be sent to her, and that he would be restored to his old rank; and I knew you would like to hear the good news from me, Zóra. But we had no reply, and then I heard of the Nawab's ill-treatment of you, and that you had escaped, and the Queen thought you might come direct to her."

"And I would have done so had I heard from Meeah," said the old man; "but I soon learned he had reached the city, and what could I have done alone?"

"Yes," observed the Padré, "we were more than a month detained on the road, as Abbas Khan's horse fell, and his wound opened again. He had a severe return of the fever, and I feared for his life. Nor did he stay when he arrived; after the combat with the Abyssinian champion, whom he slew, the Queen sent him to the army, and I hear he has returned to-day."

"Yes, and we have seen him," said Zóra; "and he brought us here. And thou art with the Queen, Maria?" she continued.

"I am with both of them, Zóra; but chiefly, by desire of Queen Chand, with the Queen Taj-ool-Nissa, whom my brother hath restored to health, and she is now strong and well. It is such a change, Zóra, and we laugh, and say the King will not know the miserable wife he left. And she has grown very dear to me, and loves to talk of you, who, she says, must be her sister. Come, shall we go to Queen Chand, she will be vexed with me if I take you not?"

"But I must change these clothes, Maria; it is not fitting for me to appear before her with these Fakeer's garments."

"On the contrary, child, she will love thee the more, and honour thee for wearing them. See, Abba, I am carrying off Zóra already," she continued, "and my brother will be security for me that I bring her back safely."

It was a strange thing to Zóra to feel herself guided through the intricate passages and corridors of the huge palace, and to see the strange deference and respect shown to Maria by all the eunuchs and Mámas on duty. At length they reached the entrance to the private apartments of the Queen Dowager, and after a brief colloquy with the eunuchs at the door, were admitted, and led to the Queen's seat by one of the women in attendance.

"Thou art welcome, Maria," she said, kindly; "but who is this thou hast brought with thee?"

"It is Zóra, your Majesty, of whom I have so often spoken. She would have taken off her Fakeer's dress; but I said I was sure she had better come as she was."

"And you were right, child. I welcome thee in the name of the King, thee and thy grandfather. By the blessed Prophet, how lovely thou art: come hither and embrace me."

What idea Zóra had previously entertained of a real Queen it is difficult to say: something very awe-inspiring, no doubt, and magnificent; but at the sight of the slight girlish figure and plain muslin dress of the great Queen whose praises were in every one's mouth, and who had held the power of the whole kingdom, Zóra became assured, and advanced to kiss the Royal lady's feet, and embrace her as she desired.

"Power of God!" cried the Queen as, having embraced Zora, she took both her cheeks in her hands and turned them alternately to the light, and looked into her soft glowing eyes; "Power of God! she is lovely, indeed, even in this poor dress. But thou hast not taken the vows, Zora?"

"No, my Queen, not yet; but when my grandfather was exalted in rank at Gulburgah I would have done so, but for a worthy lady of Golconda, who would not allow me."

"And she was right, child," returned the Queen; "such vows only belong to widows and devotees; but thou, may God forgive the thought, art neither one nor other; and if the blessing of

Chand Beebee avail aught, she will live to see thy children about thy knees;" and, stretching forth both her hands, she placed them upon Zóra's head, praying for her welfare. Then Zóra sat down and told her what had befallen her since the time that Osman Beg carried her off, and the escapes she had had, particularly the last. How her grandfather attained the rank of Wallee; and, in short, all the story we know up to the events of the morning.

"Remember that thou art my guest," said the Queen, as she dismissed Zóra; "and thou shalt want for nothing. Perhaps," she added, "thou mayest be required to-morrow at the durbar, for Osman Beg hath arrived in custody, and there may be need of thy evidence, should he deny what is alleged against him. Thou wilt not be afraid of the King's presence and the durbar?"

"I am only a poor weak girl," said Zóra, casting down her eyes; "but I have never yet been ashamed before God or man, and have no reason to fear the King or the durbar. But I have forgiven the Nawab freely. I have no claim upon him or against him; I have left all to the good Alla to judge between us. Yet, lady, had not my poor friends Runga and Burma Naik, whom I have known since I was a child, rescued me, I had surely been despoiled of my honour, and become an outcast. Now, blessed be the Lord, I can stand before my lord the King, or you, gracious lady, without shame, or a thought of shame. Forgive me that I speak so freely, lady ; but thou art as a mother to me, and my tears and my thoughts well up together without restraint. I know none of the manners of a court, for hitherto I have been secluded, and my speech may appear curt and abrupt ; but my thoughts are not so—indeed, indeed, they are as a child's before its mother."

"Thy speech is good courtly Persian, at which I marvel, child," returned the Queen, "and thou needest not be ashamed of it, Zóra ; and thy fearlessness doth thee honour. Yes, I will be thy mother truly ; and though thou mayest have forgiven thine enemy, the State hath not, and it is not seeming that such acts as Osman Beg's should be passed by unnoticed. Now depart, both of ye, for I hear the kettledrums from the city, and I have much to do ere the King enters. Bid thy grandfather eat something and be ready, for I have no doubt he will be sent for soon after His Majesty arrives."

As they passed the entrance to the young Queen's apartments, Maria asked whether they might be admitted ; but it was too late ; the Queen was in the bath, and her attiring would scarcely be finished before the King arrived. Then they went down to the old man and his friend, whom they found deeply engaged in the discussion of the young Queen's ailments ; and in the Padré's treatment of the case the old physician heartily agreed. Zóra delivered the Queen's message, and after a bath, which Ahmed had prepared, the Wallee's costly robe of honour and his crown were put on him. Zóra had changed her tunic for one of her simple woman's dresses, and they sat enjoying pleasant converse in regard to the past, while the salvoes of cannon, braying of trumpets, and loud nobat music playing on the terrace above, announced to them the arrival of the King.

Nor had they to wait long. Another salute from a battery of cannon before the Hall of Audience announced that he had taken his seat ; and two of the gold mace-bearers in waiting arrived to request the attendance of His Holiness Luteef Shah Wallee as soon as possible. And then the old man rose, and, led by Zóra, whom he declared must guide him, passed by the lower corridors into the great hall. It was a strange sight to the nobles and commanders assembled there, to see the venerable man led by the simply, not to say coarsely, dressed girl to a seat apart from the rest, and near the group of holy men who had already taken their places. All rose in deference to the new comer, whose rank was indeed superior to that of any there ; but he was spared the difficulty of performing any act of reverence to the King himself, who, rising, went to him, while Zóra fell back under charge of one of the mace-bearers, an elderly eunuch, who took care of her ; but she could see and hear perfectly whatever passed.

"We have sent for thee, illustrious Syud," said the King, as soon as silence was enforced—for the murmur of astonishment and pity had been loud and full of emotion—"to do an act of justice, which shall mark this happy day with a deed peculiar to itself. We had heard of the illustrious Syud before from Abbas Khan, who was for a time at Juldroog, and we had vowed to send for him. But, lo! as if by a miracle, or the direct interposition of the Most High, as we entered the city gate, we found him present before us. In the humble garb of Fakeers he and his granddaughter appeared by the wayside, and he fell at our horse's feet. The just and Almighty Alla had, by a strange course of circumstances, guided them to our feet, not as they were in their exile, but with increased glory and honour; for at Gulburgah the Prince Geesoo Duráz, with other princes and learned doctors of Islam, had conferred upon him, in regard to his power over men's minds, his learning, and piety, the spiritual rank of Wallee; and as such, we ourselves, as we vowed, present him to you, O friends and brothers in the faith, and pray you to do him reverence, as we ourselves do, in the presence of ye all; for the Lord hath brought to us in honour one whom our ancestor Ibrahim—may peace be on his memory!—blinded and cast out to exile, where he was forgotten and might have died, but for the aid of Him in whose service his life had passed."

Then many wept. Many who had known the old man in his prosperity, and thought him dead, pressed forward with tears and quivering features to grasp his hand once more, and kiss his feet; while cries of "Deen! Deen! A miracle! a miracle! May the saint live in peace and honour!" rose from all parts of the vast hall, and were taken up without with an enthusiasm which spread among the people even to the far ends of the city; and men saluted each other with the message of peace and the blessing of God, and the cry, "The sin of the State has been removed, let us be thankful."

When the tumult had subsided, the King, standing on the step of the throne, cried again with a loud voice, and said: "Know all men, and brothers in Islam present, that before food or water hath passed our lips to-day, we freely and entirely revoke the cruel sentence passed on the illustrious Syud Ahmed Ali, now Syud Luteef Shah Wallee. We implore, in the name of our ancestor, forgiveness for the shame and pain he hath endured for forty years, and pray him to intercede with Alla the Most High, and His holy messenger, to wipe out this sin, and remove it for ever from us and our people. We further establish this our illustrious saint in all the possessions and estates which were granted before; and we give, in addition to these, the pergunna of Kokutnoor, the scene of his child's delivery from violence. So let it be. Ameen! Ameen!" Nor was a soul present who did not cry "Ameen! Ameen!"

"Zóra! Zóra!" cried the old man, who was trembling with excitement, and feeling about with his hands, "raise me up and support me, else I cannot speak. Zóra, the Lord hath won the victory for us, and there is no longer aught hid from thee, O my child. Let her come to me, Sir, for I need her aid;" and there was a way opened for her, and he felt the soft warm hand steal into his, whilst her gentle "I am with thee, Abba," assured him. A strange sight was it to all that gorgeous assembly; the venerable old man leaning on the shoulder of the slight girl. He, clad in his rich saint's robe, and his crown with which he had been crowned; Zóra in her humble dress of soosi, and her plain muslin scarf now covering her face. But she was calm and dignified, and her modest self-possession struck those who saw her with wonder and admiration.

Then the old man stretched forth his hands and blessed the King, and the Queen who sat above, and all the people. "What can I say, my King?" he cried; "what can I say? My poor speech is dumb, but my heart goeth forth to thee and thine, and to all present who behold me. As I came hither, O King, I rested at Gogi, and distributed Fatehas at all thy ancestors' tombs; but my heart was hot and hard and sore within me, and I was about to pass King Ibrahim's tomb, when God sent me a rebuke by the mouth of this poor child: 'Forgive him,' she cried, 'forgive him; go not away from this place till thou hast forgiven him;' and I kneeled down by his tomb, struck by remorse, and bared my head, and cast dust upon it, and cried, 'I forgive thee, O Royal master, all thou didst to me, and may it be forgiven to thee in the day of judgment.' And my heart was softened, and I was accepted at Gulburgah because I preached peace to the people, as, Inshalla, I will do here, and there will be no more war or trouble. And now, O King, bid me depart home to rest, for I am old, and the events of this day have overpowered me."

Then the King ordered the ushers to bring a robe of honour, and he put it on the old man with his own hands, and hung a valuable string of pearls round his neck, to serve as prayer beads, while the people around the hall still cried blessings on them! and Zóra heard voices in the Queen's balcony crying, "Ameen; Ameen!" with, as she thought, Maria's blending with them, and sobbing too. While she led her grandfather back towards their apartments, Zóra hitherto had been able to repress her emotion, but finding Maria already there, she fell on her neck and wept passionately. She felt not only thankful for the honour accorded to Abba, but for what spoke to her heart more deeply and fondly, that Abbas Khan, and a noble old officer, whom she supposed to be his uncle, had been looking at her all the time. Nay, had she not heard their cries of joy and congratulations rising high above all others! And, late in the day, Meeah brought his uncle, and they kissed the old man's feet, and delivered the King's command that he should attend the great durbar on the morrow at noon. But Zóra had retired; she dared not look on them.

## CHAPTER III.

### THE TRIAL.

SOMEWHAT before noon on the following day the tall, burly figure of a man, who wore a dress of red cotton cloth, advanced slowly over the short turfy sward which lay beneath some huge adansonia trees in the fort. They were situated at some little distance from the gate of the citadel, by themselves, with no buildings near them, for the spot was considered impure and unholy, being, in fact, the usual place of execution in Beejapoor. A few persons were following him, and as he stopped and seated himself in the shade of one of the trees, some of those who had gathered round him began to question him as to what was to happen, for the executioner rarely made his appearance in his official costume unless some event were to follow.

"Who is it to-day, Khan Sahib?" asked one of the bystanders, with an expressive jerk of his head. "Who is to be sent to Paradise or to Hell? Nothing has happened for a long time past, but now the King has come again, thy hands will be full of work."

"Yes, brothers," returned the grim functionary; "while Queen

Chand was in authority, there was no business. She is a great deal too kind and compassionate, and she cheated me out of one fellow who was bigger than I, and the greatest bully and villain in Beejapoor, by letting that brisk young fellow, Abbas Khan, kill him. Now I should like to have slain that devil, because he was too mean for the young Khan to meddle with, and he was always mocking me and scoffing at my sword, which, he said, was nothing in comparison to his 'kussab,' as he called it, which I ought to have had also, but the Kotwal has taken it. Now look, friends, can anything be more beautiful than this?" and, rising, he drew from its scabbard a broad-bladed sword, rather broader at the point than at the hilt, with a point nearly square, with some, to him, strange-looking letters upon it, which he believed to be a charm. The motto, indeed, was—

"Inter arma silent leges,"

and the sword had been forged in Germany. "All I know is, friends, that the blade is a true 'Allemagne;' and though it is as sharp as any razor, and I got Daood Sahib, the King's armourer, to retouch the edge to-day, there will not be even a notch in it when I have done my work, and not a cloud on its fair polish. Ah, sirs, that 'kussab' of the Abyssinian's is a brutal weapon, to be used but by main strength; whereas this, my Allemagne, requires only skill, and when any great person is made over to me, I use it and no other."

"Then it is some great person, Khan Sahib, who will go to judgment to-day?"

"Nay, friends, I know not," returned the executioner. "Some one belonging to the Prince Ismail's affair was brought from the south in a palanquin which was fastened up; and I know pretty well, when Hyat Khan sends me word to go to the trees and remain there, what that means. Now, go away, all of ye, for no one must see this put into its scabbard, lest an evil glance fall on it. My art is vain, unless the edge be keen and firm. Away with ye all, I would be left to my prayers and meditations. When ye see the palanquin come out of the gate yonder, ye can return if ye will, and see what I do." And when all around him had gone, the man put the blade of his sword to his forehead and chest reverently, made a salaam to it, and slowly and carefully replaced it in its richly embroidered velvet scabbard; and as the muezzins of the neighbouring mosques sang the mid-day call to prayer, spread his waist-belt on the green sward, and performed his devotions, for the executioner was a devout man, careful in the stated observances of his faith.

The citadel was now a busier scene than when Queen Chand acted as Regent in the absence of the King. There were so many more dignitaries to be received, so much relating to the army to be arranged, so many rewards and dresses of honour to be distributed, that the approaches to the palace were always crowded.

This did not affect our friends in the least, as they were not only pleasantly secluded, but at such a distance from the exciting crowds and turmoil, that they saw none of it, and heard only a little. At the council of the night before, all the public accounts for the period of Queen Chand's administration, which had been prepared beforehand, were read to the King, and duly audited. Many new patents of nobility as rewards for service, and grants of estates, were ordered to be drafted, Syud Luteef Shah Wallee's among the number. And we are glad to record also, that not only Abbas Khan, now created Khan Bahadoor, and commander of five thousand, but Runga Naik was received into the lower grade of nobility, and created lord of twenty villages near his own ancestral estate of Korikul, and was to receive a dress of honour in full Court. Assuredly his service had not been in vain, while other rewards, in proportion to their merits, were allotted to his brave followers. But all these were minor points; the business assigned to the morrow was of a much more important nature, for as they sat in the council hall, Hyat Khan, the Kotwal, announced to the King that Osman Beg, the Governor of Juldroog, had arrived as a prisoner, and asked how he should be disposed of. The Queen Chand, who was sitting beside her nephew, said, "Son, I claim thy attention to this case first, for it is of grave importance to many that the truth should be made manifest to all, and justice be done. We would have seen to it ourselves when you were absent, but we thought thou shouldst decide upon it. It is a painful case, but justice must be done."

"Certainly, and without favour, aunt. Yet why not by thee? Is there any power thou dost not share with me? Is there any order of thine to which I do not bow? Yet"—for the Queen was waving her hand in deprecation of his expressions—"yet, if thou wilt, I will be present with thee, and we will share the task together. Let the prisoner be well lodged and cared for, Khan Sahib," he continued to Hyat Khan; "let his arrival be announced to his father, who may visit him, and let him be present to-morrow at the afternoon durbar, when we shall be at leisure."

And now the time had come. The King as he rose had received many persons of rank, and transacted his usual business with the Ministers. He then retired for awhile; but, after the noon-day prayer, had entered the great hall of audience, and, due proclamation having been made within and without, he took his seat on the Royal throne, which had now been properly arranged. This was, in fact, a broad, low, wooden stool, with cushions of rich velvet, with a back also of wood, both being covered with thin plates of gold, inlaid, especially the back and canopy, with very rare and valuable precious stones, arranged in ingenious patterns. Queen Chand sat by her nephew, on her usual seat or cushion of velvet, and dressed in her usual simple fashion; but the King, though he wore white muslin only, had a precious jewel in his turban, and a necklace of large diamonds and emeralds, which flashed brightly whenever he moved. Before him lay a light Court sword, in a purple velvet sheath. He looked younger, as indeed he was by three years, than Abbas Khan, who, with other officers of the private Court, stood rather behind and to one side of the Royal daïs; but he was of slighter make, while his features, though delicate, were of darker colour than those of Abbas Khan, whose complexion was almost ruddy.

A little lower, on the first broad step or platform of the daïs, sat the old Syud, Luteef Shah Wallee, in the place of honour nearest to the King and Queen; and just behind him, indeed touching him, the slight form of Zóra, dressed in her ordinary coarse garb, was seen covering her face as well as she could from the earnest and curious glances of those who were wondering, as before, at her presence among so large a company of men. Behind her was the priest, Francis d'Almeida, who cheered her every now and then; but his sister, for whom Zóra was longing, sat above in the Queen's balcony with the other ladies-in-waiting and servants. The hall itself appeared the same as on the first day we saw it, except that the dresses of the courtiers were not of a military character, but of simple white muslin, crossed by a baldrick of gold lace or tissue, which was intended to hold a sword; but such weapons were carried in the hand, while a knife or dagger with jewelled hilt was stuck into the muslin girdle.

When all the presentations had concluded, the King, having had silence proclaimed, spoke with a firm voice, and said, "Listen, O ye nobles and Ministers of the State! Sundry accusations have been made against Osman Beg, son of the brave Sooltan Beg, and we have caused him to be present here, before us, before the law officers of the State, and before his equals and superiors in rank. Let no one, therefore, say that this investigation was held secretly, or otherwise than in the sight of the Lord on high, and the day-beams of justice. Let, therefore, Osman Beg be brought hither, and let him reply to these accusations."

The old Syud could not see him, we know, but he stood directly in front of Zóra as he entered, accompanied by a party of the Kotwal's guards, and proclamation was made by the Mohur that Osman Beg, Turcoman, stood before the throne. The prisoner then made a deep obeisance to the King and Queen, which was not returned by either, but to those assembled he made no gesture of salute. He looked round defiantly as he crossed his arms, and then, letting them drop to his sides, again saluted the King slightly, and said with a firm voice, "I am present, O King, to hear any accusation."

At the sound of his well-remembered tones Zóra shuddered, for the events of the last night she had seen him were too fresh in her memory to be forgotten. But it was not a shudder of fear, it was rather a repellent action as against a foul reptile, and her cheeks flushed, and her tiny white teeth were set as if in resolution.

Then the chief Kazee spoke from his seat, and said, "This is a case of treachery, O King, against thee, and thy person, kingdom, and security. These letters were found on the person of the Abyssinian slain in the combat of ordeal, and are addressed to Elias Khan, who died in battle. Osman Beg, in the name of the King, I ask thee if these are truly thine own ; look at them."

Osman Beg was not allowed to touch them, but they were held near his face and turned in every possible direction. There were many of them, the date and purport of each being read aloud by a scribe present.

What could he do or say? the writing was sometimes his own, sometimes that of his confidential scribe. All the seals were his, and corresponded exactly with that he wore on his finger as a ring. He appeared to become weary of these documents being read, and handed about to receive the criticisms of others ; and, with an impatient exclamation, for which he was reproved by the ushers, and admonished to be more respectful, he said, "Do not trouble yourself, Kazee Sahib, the letters are all mine ; I deny them not."

"Then I will read one, only one, for His Majesty to hear," was the reply; and, standing up, the Kazee selected one and read it so that all could hear. It was to Elias Khan, stating that the Padré at Moodgul, Dom Diego, had agreed to all conditions; that three thousand Europeans were ready at Goa; and that when Eyn-ool-Moolk was prepared he should deliver over the fort to any officers they might send, when he would join them; and, having overpowered Abbas Khan's detachment, they would march rapidly upon Beejapoor, put Chand Beebee to death, and take possession of the treasury and the capital; while another party, led by himself or Elias Khan, should pursue the King and bring him to Beejapoor, or execute him in camp, as might be most expedient.

The Kazee could read no more, for there arose a shout in the assembly of "Let the traitor die! Send for the executioner! Away with him!"

But Osman Beg turned in defiance to them all. "Dogs!" he cried, "all this would have been, and more, had Eyn-ool-Moolk not been slain, as Elias Khan was, by treachery. Ay! and ye know it, one and all of this assembly. What I have done, I have done; and what has happened is my fate. Yes, if ye wish to know what the Padré at Moodgul did, and wanted to do, get some one to read his letters. He was a brave fellow that, and would have struck in for us. Very different from the other, who, I hear, is in Beejapoor; he was too great a coward to be a traitor."

"He confesses before the King, and before God and men, that he was prepared to do all that is written in these letters by his own hand; and the law is that the punishment is death," cried the Kazee.

"My lord! my King!" cried Abbas Khan, as he saw the King was about to speak; and had he declared judgment, there would have been no delay in execution, "I cry for mercy and pardon. When I was ill and near to death in Juldroog he was kind to me; he not only gave me protection, but attended me as a brother. My King, he is my cousin, and we have played together when we were children; nor was my King absent. For the sake of his noble father, spare his life!"

Osman Beg answered not a word. He stood, as he had done hitherto, with his arms crossed defiantly, looking now to the Kazee, now to the King, and now to his cousin, apparently defying all.

"Of a truth thou deservest death, Osman Beg. Thou wouldst have, by thine own writing, put my venerable aunt, beloved of all" —and the people cried "Ameen! Ameen!"—"to a cruel death. Thou wouldst have slain me and thy cousin, Abbas Khan; and thou wouldst have prolonged war and misery in our kingdom. But it pleased Alla, the just and merciful, to frustrate all thy plots, and to bring them to naught; and for the sake of thine aged father, who fought beside Humeed Khan in the last desperate fight, and, when others fled, refused to fly with them, and still rallied men round his standard, we, in the name of the Most High, whose Regent we are over this people, give thee thy life; for He hath spared His servant through fields of carnage; and we would not, on the first day of taking our seat on the throne of our ancestors, stain it with blood. But thou art disgraced; thy rank and thy estates are confiscated; and thou canst stay here no longer. If thou, Osman Beg, returnest under any pretence, remember, the Kazee's just sentence shall at once be carried out. Hyat Khan, see that he be removed and banished, conducted ten coss beyond the frontier, and let to go whither he will."

Osman Beg did not move. He glared around him with defiance still, and, looking at the King, cried out, "I go, as thou wilt have it, King Ibrahim; nor will I return to disgrace and dishonour. But, before I depart, I claim justice at thy hands, justice which thy meanest subjects may claim from thee. Give me my wife. Take honour, rank, estates, what thou wilt, but give me my wife whom I see sitting there with the Dervish of Juldroog. There!" he shouted, as he pointed his finger at Zóra; "there! she is mine by the law, and I claim her under the law. Give her to me and I depart, and leave only my curse behind me."

Then arose another shout, more fierce, more prolonged than

the first. "He has forfeited clemency; he has insulted the holy saint. Let him die!"

"Is it so, Huzrut?" said the King, addressing himself to the old Syud, as soon as silence had been proclaimed; "is it so? Speak, or let the child speak. Fear not, maiden," he continued, in a soothing voice to Zóra; "thou art in God's presence, and the King's; speak as thou wouldst do, and wilt do, in the day of judgment."

"I have no complaint against him, my lord," replied the Syud. "For what he did to my child when we were under him at Juldroog, he will answer to God, who mercifully protected and delivered my child and me from cruelty and insults. All that is past now, and we are here in safety; and, for my own part, he is now forgiven. I say, then, leave him to the Lord's will. Ask her, she will not be ashamed to say the truth, even in the midst of thousands of men. Rise, then, Zóra, and the Lord will give thee strength, my child. Thou art a Syud, and a Syud's honour trembles not before righteous judges. Men will not so much as look at thee, child; for a Syud's honour is as precious to them as it is to me and thyself."

"Fear not, Zóra-bee," said the King, gently, "we are all thy grandfather's friends and thine; but Osman Beg hath demanded thee as his wife, and should have his reply from thyself, for thy honour's sake. Speak, and fear not."

Zóra had trembled with shame and indignation as Osman Beg made his demand, at once so appalling and disgraceful to her. Her breast heaved with sobs, her eyes grew hot, and scalding tears fell from them over her burning cheeks. She felt as though she would have choked and died. But the girl's undaunted courage did not fail her even in that dire extremity, and the solemn adjuration of her grandfather and the gentle words of the King stimulated her and assured her; and hastily brushing away the tears which still glistened on her cheeks, and murmuring a silent prayer, she rose to her feet with a calmness she had little expected, and a kind of dread silence fell on the assembly at a scene so novel and so strange. Above, in the Queen's balcony, she heard a low clapping of hands, which gave her courage; and the Queen Dowager's encouragement of "Fear not, daughter, no harm can come to thee," was timidly acknowledged by a grateful look and reverence.

As she cast her eyes around, she saw that men's faces were averted from her, and many heads bowed down; but opposite to her stood Abbas Khan, his features quivering with excitement, and his eyes as if striving to catch hers and give her strength; while near the centre of the hall stood Osman Beg, glaring on her defiantly, with a horrible expression of anticipated triumph, which thrilled through her, but from which she did not blench.

Those who saw her remembered for years afterwards the simple, modest figure, dressed in clothes hardly better than those of a peasant, and the beautiful but excited face of the maiden. And those who did not dare to look on her, heard only the tones of her soft musical voice, which penetrated to every ear, and, indeed, to every heart of the many who heard it.

"Before the Lord God, and ye who hear me," she said, slowly, "I am not his wife; and I have witnesses that I am not. I see the Moolla of Juldroog, who has known me from my birth, sitting yonder. Let him speak, if he be allowed." And as the King assented and signed to him, the old man rose.

"It is the truth, O King and brethren. I was summoned before the Nawab one evening to perform a nika between him and Zóra-bee, which I thought strange. But I found the whole affair a mockery, and a shameful violation of all law and custom. Zóra was imprisoned under charge of two women from Moodgul, and I called for her in vain. Osman Beg dare not produce her. There was no one to represent her. And to expect me, a humble priest of God, to perform a mock marriage to cover his violence, was an insult to me; and I rose and left the assembly, every respectable person in it accompanying me and guarding me. Next day messengers were sent in every direction to obtain a Moolla, but none arrived until Zóra-bee and the old Syud had escaped. There was no marriage, O King and brethren; and he lies before God who says there was."

"He lies!" cried Osman Beg, furiously; "he lies. She, standing there shamelessly, had come to me before, and what I did was to save her shame—the shame of a holy Syud, whom I respected."

This pitiless speech affected the assembly deeply. The Moolla's evidence had carried conviction to every heart; but was this terrible accusation true? Some even seemed to lose faith in the girl, but her faculties were now strung to the highest tension, and her spirit seemed to rise with the increasing danger of her situation, as she cried,—

"He says I am shameless, and that I came to him of my own will. Let his slave Jooma, who stands yonder, say what happened."

Jooma, who with other witnesses had been brought from Juldroog, being now called by the usher, stepped forward and made a humble prostration; then rose, and joining his hands, said,—

"Let my master do me no harm, O King, and I will speak the truth."

"No one can harm thee," replied the Kazee for the King. "Speak truly, and without fear."

"He," and he pointed to Osman Beg, "had often asked me to bring Zóra-bee to him; but I had played with the child, and gathered flowers for her, and I always refused; and he threatened me. One day he ordered two other slaves like me to bring her, and when they refused, he drew his sword and slew one, and a eunuch, who has run away, killed the other; and their bodies were flung into a hole in the rocks, and are there still. Their blood was wet on the rocks when he sent for me, and he had his bloody sword in his hand. 'Go, and bring Zóra,' he said, 'else thou shalt die!' And I was afraid; God forgive me for being afraid, and I bowed my head, and said, 'On my head and eyes be it.' And I took another slave with me, who knew nothing about it; and we went to watch for the girl, and saw her come to the bastion she loved, with Ahmed. Then we went down to them, and I sent Ahmed away on a false message. Zóra was never afraid of me. When Ahmed was gone, I seized her, and she screamed; and I tied her up with my waist-band, and we took her to the palace in a black blanket; and I carried her in my arms, and laid her down on a bed where the Mámas were. Oh, my lord King, I did wrong," continued the man, blubbering, as he cast himself on the ground; "and if Zóra is to die, kill me also, for it was I that did all the mischief. Not anyone else but me, because he said he would slay me as he had slain the others. Their bones are in the hole, and the new Killadar tried to get them out, but he could not. Ask him."

"As if a master could not slay an insolent slave whom he had bought with his own money," cried Osman Beg, scornfully. "And can such as he be believed against a true Moslem's word? I say he lies, there was no force; and she came when I sent him to call her."

It was well for Zóra, then, that Osman Beg's cook, whom we may remember, had also been brought. She now stepped forward, and said, simply, "Jooma speaks the truth; Zóra-bee was brought into the harem tied up in a blanket, and I saw Máma Luteefa and her servant untying her. I went from the kitchen to look, as every one was saying the Nawab had had Zóra carried off, and was going to marry her; and I was ordered to cook pilao for the company. And, for the matter of that," continued the old woman, as she looked round confidently, as many cries of "Shahbash! well done!" fell on her ears, "every one in the palace knew it; every one in the fort. Why, I could name a score, yea, a hundred, who knew it too. Why don't they speak out like me? His wife, indeed! She was as much married to him as I was; and she is as pure now as when she was born. Does the Nawab think any one could have come to him without my knowledge? Shookr! he should be beaten on the mouth with a shoe for all he is a Nawab. Ask Goolab-bee, the pán woman; she was with Zóra and the two Mámas of Moodgul all the night Zóra was carried off by Runga Naik, and kept her safely as her own child."

"We need hear no more, my friends," said the King. "For my own part I am satisfied. Yet I ask her once more if she hath aught to adduce?"

"Only these papers," she said, timidly, "which my grandfather told me to preserve. This is the letter he wrote, and sent by Máma Luteefa to Korikul. It bears his seal, and is in his own hand; and he says he will come to us and have the marriage done. The second is the deed he gave to the robber who had instructions to carry me off from Kukeyra, and who was killed; and with it is also the letter he wrote to the Kazee of Kembavee, asking him to come and marry me to him. Oh, my King and my lord, why should he have selected me, a poor orphan and a Fakeer, for this persecution, from which the Lord saved me many times? Even at Kokutnoor I had not escaped from the robbers but for the heavy rain that the Lord sent. If I had been guilty and shameless, as he declares I was, would the Lord have helped me? If I had been married to him, as he declares, why ask for me again? Why ask the good Kazee of Kembavee to marry him to me? I am ashamed to speak so much," she continued, timidly, "but her honour is dearer to a Syud's child than her life. I had not thought to complain, and I make no complaint. I have forgiven him freely, as I forgive him now; and I would have been silent, but when he said I was shameless, could I be silent? I have no father, no mother, my lord, but you and the Queen. I am but a poor orphan crying to you both for justice before the Lord."

The reading of the several papers produced had, to all appearance, silenced Osman Beg, and his head drooped on his chest despairingly; yet still, beaten back on every point, he made one more last effort.

"If I produce the Moolla who married me," he said, scornfully, "will ye be content? Stand forth, Moolla Aboo Bukr, and speak for me."

"I, your slave, will speak the truth, master," he said, removing the false beard he wore; and then prostrating himself before the King, cried, "May I be your sacrifice, O King, but I am not even one of the faithful; I am only a Hindoo, a poor buffoon, who frequents marriages and festivals, and tries to amuse people. The night Zóra-bee was to be married, and when thy servant found the Moolla walked away in a huff, and we sat looking at each other like owls, I clapped on my beard and wagged it, and said, 'Good people, let me marry them;' and, God pardon me, I tried to recite ——"

"Enough! enough! this is no time or place for thy buffoonery," cried the King, who, however grave the occasion, could hardly keep his countenance. "Away from the presence. Is the Khan mad, mother, that he tried this last resource?"

"I know not," said the Queen; "but I long to embrace that brave child, who shall be as a daughter to me henceforth." The Queen had been sobbing as she sat, and her face was wet with tears. "Come to me, Zóra," she said gently to her, "and I will acknowledge thee before them;" and the girl, who had sat down weeping tears which soothed and relieved her, whispered to her grandfather that the Queen needed her, and rising, passed behind the throne to the Queen Dowager's seat; and the Royal lady, placing her hands on the girl's head, rose up, and said to all present, as Zóra stood beside her, "This child the Lord hath preserved from danger and ruin, and she is pure, and a holy Syudanee. She is an orphan, moreover, and her revered grandfather, Syud Luteef Shah Wallee, is old and infirm. Therefore, we, our lord the King and myself, adopt her as our daughter, and will marry her honourably in her own rank. As for that man," and she pointed to Osman Beg, "my lord the King will deal with him as he deserves." And then once more the great hall rung with cries of "Justice is done! May Chand Beebee live a hundred years!" "Hear the gracious words she speaks!" and the like; till, at a signal from the King, the usher again enforced silence. But before he could speak, an aged man, whose figure was still firm and erect, rose, and advanced to the foot of the throne, where, after prostrating himself and kissing the King's feet, he took the sword he had carried in his hand, and laying it in his muslin handkerchief, offered it to the King. It was Adam Khan, Turcoman, the father of Osman, who thus spoke in broken accents,—

"Say no more, my lord and my King. Spare me, the aged servant of thy house, one who was serving Ibrahim Adil Shah when the venerable Syud suffered. Say no more, for my honour's sake, for I have fought and bled for thee. I speak not for him, my unworthy son; but I admit his guilt against you, my lord, and my Queen, and against that poor orphan, whose father served under me, and died in battle. Yea, my lord, and my Queen, I admit the guilt freely, and ye have been witness to its proof. So justice has been done before the Lord, and though I suffer, I rejoice. Now, therefore, my King, if thou hast given this wretch his life, let us go. I have no tie to life, nor children, nor wife, nor any one. Let us go, then, to Mecca, where he may pray for pardon to the Messenger, who will accept his penitence. The ship from Choule is about to sail, and we will depart, and our shame and dishonour may be forgiven. But take this poor memorial of the service of one who hath been faithful, whom thy Royal mother knoweth to be faithful. I leave to thee the estates I hold, but, with permission, all my command with the horses and men I give to Abbas Khan, nephew of the brave Humeed Khan."

"Peace, father!" said his son; "humble thyself no more. One more chance of justice is open to all. Hath this girl any champion to undertake her defence? Men's tongues are swayed by a breath of opinion, but sharp steel is the true arbiter. Again, therefore, I claim her as my wife, let who will be her champion."

Then a number of fiery young men started up; but among them all Abbas Khan was the calmest, stateliest, and most remarkable. "I owe my life to that poor orphan," he said, "and I should be unworthy if I refused her aid in her need. Listen, Osman Beg; though I have partaken of thy hospitality, thou must accept me in the ordeal if thou persist in claiming her."

"I accept!" cried Osman Beg. "On foot or horseback, with armour or without, I claim thee, and thee only. The day is yet young, the field where the Abyssinian died is open. Come! thou art welcome; and if thou refuse, thou art a coward and a liar!"

"Silence!" cried the King, angrily; "an honourable man can only fight with one of equal honour. Thou, Osman Beg, art one whose life hath been far-famed for treachery; whose honour hath yielded before falsehood, and become a thing for honest men to spit on. Away! go to the holy Kibleh with thine honoured father; haply the Lord may give thee grace to repent. Champion! nay, she needeth none; hath not the Lord been her champion in preserving her from thee? Hyat Khan, remove him; see that he is guarded and escorted with his father to the ship for Mecca."

"It is my destiny," murmured Osman Beg, as he retreated. "Must I go? But I will not cease to pursue her while I have life; and my revenge will only sleep, only sleep."

"And now, sirs, we have detained you long," said the King; "but we dismiss ye with our thanks, and grateful to the Lord, also, that He hath manifested His justice in the protection of an orphan child."

Till the Queen rose, Zóra had been sitting beside her, but her mind was in a strange condition. What she had said, how the people had clapped their hands and shouted for her; how she had escaped from the deadly danger, worse than death, which had threatened her; what the King and Queen Chand had said to her, of all this she knew very little; but when Meeah, as she loved to think of him, rose up, and before all the assembled people declared he was her champion, her heart swelled almost to bursting, and she could only look at him with wistful eyes, while her cheeks burned painfully and her breath came in gasps. Meeah! he was true; he had not forgotten the night watch. Meeah! he would have risked his life for her honour. Oh that she could throw herself at his feet and clasp his knees, and say—— Ah! what could she have said, but that she loved him, that she would die for him, if needs be.

She was anxious to be alone, to pray and thank God in her own simple fashion, to send Fatehas to all the saints' shrines; and pleading her duty to her grandfather, the good Queen, perceiving the girl was well nigh distraught, bid her go, and she would send for her presently. And Zóra, leading the old man forth, regained their apartments quietly. And when he was seated in his old place, and had drunk some cool sherbet, he drew her to him, and said, "Child, remember this day; 'tis the end of my Turreequt, except the last when the angel calls me; but it is the beginning of thine in honour and joy. When that youth spoke, my heart leaped towards him; and, if the Lord will, he may lead thee to eternal peace."

Zóra could not reply, her heart was too full; and how could she mention Meeah? Maria came in soon after, with her brother; and while the good Padré stayed with his old friend, Zóra and Maria withdrew to Zóra's apartment, and in a burst of softening tears, the girl's overcharged spirit was relieved. Never before had Maria heard the history of Zóra's abduction and escape, and she was amazed at the girl's endurance and bravery. Then Maria took her to the Queen Chand, who laid her head on her own bosom, and comforted her.

"Thou art my daughter, now," she said, "for thou art brave and true; and I will be to thee a mother, grateful that God hath sent me such a child to love, and to be beloved by. Nay, I will not take thee from thy Abba, for without thee he cannot live; but I shall see thee daily, and there need be no reserve between us." Nor was there from thenceforth.

* * * * * * *

Under the adansonian trees the executioner had sat waiting, until their broad shadows stretched across the sward and were becoming longer. At last a messenger came and said—

"Get up, O Khan, no one comes to thee to-day, and Hyat Khan bids thee go home."

"Hai! hai! alas! alas!" said the functionary, with a sigh. "And thou wert so sharp, my son;" and he once more drew his weapon from its sheath. "He would never have felt it. Well, so let the King have mercy; and yet thy time will come again some day or other, O my son. Well, thou shalt be ready;" and with a sigh he made a deep salaam to the glittering weapon, and, returning it to its sheath, covered the sword with his scarf, and walked slowly towards the city.

## CHAPTER IV.

### FREEDOM.

AND now there was rest and peace; but how different to that in the old fort, to which Zóra's mind often wandered. How different grew on her day by day, more and more. Instead of the dreamy, uneventful life she used to lead, there was now excitement and active employment. Her constant attendance on her grandfather never relaxed; and he was perhaps more exacting than before—partly on account of his increasing infirmity, and partly because of the strange and new consciousness of increased dignity and importance which was growing upon him, and which was foreign to his naturally humble temperament. His devotional exercises, too, in which he was assisted by some of the priests of the city mosques, were much prolonged; and he was often weary and peevish, and on such occasions the presence of old Mamoolla and Ahmed only provoked him, and Zóra became indispensable. Had he not, also, been invited to preach in the Jooma Mosque, where six thousand men of all ranks sat with the King to listen to him on the occasion of the King's first visit to that noble building, when he went to return thanks for the close of the war? He knew that he had moved many hearts; for though he lauded patriotism and bravery in war, yet he dwelt more strongly and more earnestly on the blessings of peace, industry, sobriety, and devotion; and these were themes which flowed from his lips spontaneously and with fervid eloquence. Many men who listened then, and afterwards, thought him inspired; and whether he spoke in the rough Dekhani dialect, or in the softer Persian, he was equally impressive. Hundreds became his devoted followers, and I fear the burly high priest's influence decreased in proportion.

From the high priest issued the hardest doctrines of Islam: the most difficult metaphysical arguments that learned commentators had ever supplied. The learning and study they displayed were wonderful, and immeasurably exceeded that of the old Dervish; but they were hard to comprehend, and to the uninitiated utterly unintelligible, whereas those of our old friend were sweet and consoling, encouraging to good works and love to men, as well as to love to God. Hence there arose two factions, as it were, in the city, which on any and every occasion were ready to divide into opposing portions; and Luteef Shah Wallee was denounced as an heretical and misleading preacher, not belonging to any saintly family, who neglected to preach damnation to unbelievers, but sought to win them by kindness, which was contrary to the texts and doctrines of the blessed Korán; and thus, when he had expected peace, our old friend found strife, which as time passed grew more bitter.

But it was pleasant, nevertheless, after such services, to receive the visits of his friends. And even some of his contemporaries, Ekhlas Khan, the blind old minister, several of the physicians and lawyers, some of the local nobility, and men of learning, enrolled themselves among his disciples, and sat at his feet, enjoying the words which fell from his lips with true zest. And as to the common people, there were many likewise, but the majority still adhered to the old *régime*; and the precincts of the Chishtee Palace and cemetery, which were in the centre of the city outside the walls, were as crowded as usual. The Chishtee priest had, too, many subordinate ministers, who gathered in his revenues from vows, oblations, and performances of ceremonials in thousands of families; and the shrine was richly endowed besides by estates and charged on many collections of revenue. But our old friend had none of these, and desired none. All he received he gave away in charity to the poor at the great mosque, and sent to other mosques in the city, and to the almshouse, and the public hospitals, and travellers' rest houses. And he had no ambition to do more; certainly none to become rich; for the King had enriched him far beyond his requirements, and collections from the estates were beginning to come in. What was he to do with them? He had no wants, for the ordinary allowance at the fort was sufficient for food and clothes, and the expense and maintenance of a household were unknown both to him and Zóra.

Zóra, too, had her separate duties, apart from those connected with her grandfather. Rising early, she frequently joined Queen Chand for the first morning prayer, and then assisted her by writing fair copies of the drafts she had made over night; and when Abba rose, she was informed of it, and was allowed to go to assist him. Sometimes she sang to the Queen the few things she knew, or did embroidery for her. And the Queen liked Zóra's beyond that of all her other maidens, and entrusted her with the finishing of a precious and costly piece in seed pearls on velvet, which was to be sent as an offering to Mecca, some of the most delicate parts of which had been done by herself. Sometimes, too, she read aloud, while the Queen worked, from such books as she had studied under her grandfather, and learned from him the proper rhythm and emphasis. And Zóra's ear was so correct, and her cadence so musical, that it was like a sweet song, or a chaunt, or a spirited declamation, as the subject required.

Every day, too, while the Queen took her noonday rest, Zóra's time was her own; and Maria came to her, and they sat under a great fig-tree which flourished in the little garden, and held sweet communion with each other, or worked. Zóra, though comparatively little time had passed, was not now the shy, simple child Maria had loved at Juldroog. She found the girl's character developed and strengthened by contact with the world without, and by the experience, rough and sad as it had been, that she had endured in the wild persecution of Osman Beg, and the society of those with whom she had come in contact since she had left the fort. Over and over again had Maria requested her to tell the story of her escape from Osman Beg's treachery and violence; and she could follow it all, from the seat on the well-remembered bastion, with the grand ravine and cataract before it, to the final scene of the trial, of which she had been a spectator from the Queen's balcony, and estimate with wonder and admiration, and with many a sympathetic tear and sob, the young girl's fortitude and endurance. She could estimate, too, Zóra's dread that she might still, by some unknown chance, fall into this ruthless man's hands; and Maria would soothe and calm her, bidding her trust in the Lord, and in the powerful friends that had been given to her. The one was a humble Christian, the other a Mussulman girl. Yet, in the sympathy and love that united them, there was nothing wanting. Sometimes, too, they now spoke of "Meeah," for Maria could not but discern, from his behaviour at the trial, that the young man loved Zóra fondly, and even passionately; and Zóra would listen to the few words Maria said on the subject with a fond and even sad interest, hiding her burning face in Maria's bosom, with secret hope and yet with trembling dread. Her one hope in life lay with him, for Abba was declining in strength, and he was over-taxing a mind and frame which had been so long unexercised, and that she knew must bring with it the inevitable consequence of death. Till that time came she declared that not even Meeah should separate her from the fondly loved old man; and Maria could understand, however great the temptation, that her vow would not be broken.

But Abbas Khan himself was not free from embarrassment in regard to taking any formal step towards Zóra. Years ago, when his uncle was by no means so rich as he was at present, and his brother, Abbas Khan's father, had been only a Silladar, or owner of a few horses in the Royal Dekhani cavalry, his little son had been betrothed to the daughter of a comrade of the same rank as himself in the army, of Abyssinian descent, but whose estates rendered his daughter, Sukeena, a desirable connection in the consideration of many families of Beejapoor, notwithstanding the report that Sukeena-bee was very forbidding both in person and features. She was, indeed, both lame and deformed; and was in addition so ugly, that she was known by a sobriquet by no means complimentary. Sukeena's mother was descended from a Nubian family, which had again intermarried with Abyssinians. But it was not from this cause alone that Sukeena's appearance was forbidding; her father was a very plain and somewhat humpbacked man; her grandmother, the daughter of one of the Abyssinian noblemen, had been only too glad to dispose of a singularly ugly daughter to a respectable man, and gave with her a dower of property which, as he said, endowed the Lady Fyzun with a beauty more precious and more lasting than that of a pretty face. From this union had resulted one daughter only, the girl who had been betrothed in her early childhood to Abbas Khan.

Neither Humeed Khan, Abbas Khan's uncle, nor his wife, the Lady Fatima, had been parties to this early betrothal. When it took place they were at a distance; but when the Lady Fatima returned to Beejapoor, her nephew's father and mother had both died. For a time, the Queen Chand had adopted the orphan boy, and he shared in the instruction of the young King; but afterwards Abbas Khan had returned to his uncle's house, and taken his place in the Royal service. Considering the connection which already existed by betrothment, it would have been impossible for the Lady Fatima to have avoided the Lady Fyzun and her daughter. Both husbands were absent at the war, with the King. Sukeena's father, notwithstanding his partial deformity, was, as is often seen to be the case, a man of immense strength and ever conspicuous bravery, and he had risen to a rank considerably higher than it was at the time of the old betrothal. In point, therefore, of social condition the families were pretty equal, though the Abyssinian lady claimed precedence in consequence of her descent from a long line of ministers and generals, who had attained rank and power in the days of the Bahmuny dynasty at Gulburgah and Beeder.

From the period of her return to Beejapoor, the Lady Fatima had been obliged to offer civilities to the Lady Fyzun, which, of course, included her daughter; and the Lady Fyzun was a woman not only of excessive pride, but of extremely sharp, disagreeable temper, and, moreover, very parsimonious. Her husband, poor man, was especially mild and good-natured, and, if he could have managed it, would have got away as far as was possible from his wife at all times. But at a season like the present, when the whole army had returned from a campaign, and there seemed to be neither possibility nor probability of the renewal of war, Zyn Khan, for that was his name, was obliged to remain at home, and to submit to his wife's conduct and remarks with all the patience and equanimity he could command. After more than two years of respite, his trials recommenced the day of the King's triumphal entry.

The Lady Fyzun was, as I have already remarked, very economical. The house-steward and the clerks who kept the house accounts could never satisfy her as to the expenditure of the cook, or the daroghas of the kitchen and stables. She was at perpetual war with them. Too much butter, or meat, or onions and garlic, or vegetables, were surely used for cooking the domestic daily food. The horses ate too much grain and fodder; the slaves and eunuchs wore out their clothes too fast. In short, these were, and had been, subjects of altercation for years, and were by no means worn out. Now the morning of the King's arrival was a fast day, though not one of a rigid character, and few, especially on an occasion like this, would have observed it at all; but Fyzun-bee had no idea of allowing laxity of religious observances. She kept the Rumzan and Mohorum with a positively fearful exactitude, and starved herself, her daughter, and her household to the very verge of endurance. On the other hand, on joyful anniversaries, when a liberal addition of savoury food was made to the daily allowance by every, even the poorest, housewife, Fyzun-bee's feast was of the smallest dimensions and humblest character. Sweetmeats were not made in the house of good sugar-candy and fresh butter, but ordered from the confectioners, who sent, according to order, the coarsest, and but little of them. In the pilao, the cook was restricted in the use of ghee, spice, and meat; camel and even buffalo flesh was used instead of good fat mutton; and the cook, who was really a mistress of her art, would, had she not been a slave, have no doubt sought a more liberal mistress in sheer vexation.

Zyn Khan had ridden with the King's throng of courtiers and officers in the entrance procession. He had attended the durbar, and had been thus detained till late in the day; he was, therefore, not only extremely tired, but hungry to boot; and though he expected no delicacies at home, yet he felt sure that there would be food at least, and perhaps the cook might do something special for him.

He had left the durbar in company with his friends Humeed Khan and Abbas Khan, and at the gate of their mansion had parted with them. Then, as they separated, Humeed Khan had said to him, good humouredly, "If the fast is observed to-day in thy house, come to us, brother; nay, stay now if thou wilt, with a hearty welcome."

Now, though only at the gate, the fragrant scent of savoury food had already reached him, for it was to be a feast for many of the inferior officers and men of Humeed Khan's household troops, which would be a warranty that there were better dishes beyond that; and Zyn Khan's hunger increased, while his mouth fairly watered. But to eat in a stranger's house just after a long absence would be a positive affront to his wife, of whom he stood in awe, and he passed on to the reception that awaited him. Certainly all the servants were at their posts. There were trays of offerings, and lighted lamps waved over him; the women servants and eunuchs chaunted a discordant welcome; but his nose was regaled by no savoury smell; and, on passing the door of the kitchen court, he looked in, and beheld the old cook and her two assistant girls sitting dolefully on the step of the kitchen itself; and as they got up and waved their arms towards him, cracking their knuckles against their cheeks, he returned the salute by crying out, "The peace of God on you, Máma Leila; I trust you have something good for your hungry master."

"On the contrary, my lord," returned the woman, with a spiteful accent; "no firewood and no food have been allowed me to-day, else thou shouldst have eaten well."

Zyn Khan was really angry. "No firewood and no food have been given Leila-bee to-day," he cried, regardless of the approach and salutation of his wife and daughter. "No food! and I have this day ridden ten coss (twenty miles), and been out in the hot sun all the time, and attended the King's durbar, without a morsel to eat. And this is my welcome after two years' absence. Fyzun! art thou not ashamed, O wife?"

"I ashamed! I, the descendant of Princes and Ministers, ashamed of keeping the holy fast, and of the service of Alla, instead of thy greedy belly. Touba! Touba! As-tagh-fur-oolla! Shame, and God forbid that I should hear such words from the father of thy daughter Sukeena! No; there is no food and no fire in the house to-day for gluttons; let them meditate on the saints, and feed on spiritual food, like true men of Islam. Be satisfied, O Khan, that I, thy wife, and thy beloved daughter, are in the same condition as thyself, fasting for the love of Alla and the saints. Thou canst bathe and refresh thyself, for hot water is ready for thee in the bath, and I will see (for the expression of his face was far from amiable) and get some confection which may stay thy hunger till night."

"Till night!" groaned Zyn Khan; "till night! Is this how

thy mother teaches thee, Sukeena-bee? I would not be thy husband, girl." These were the first words he had spoken to her, and as he uttered them he looked over the ungainly, crooked form, the sour, ugly features, and the really mean clothing of his daughter. In his heart he compared her to the simple, lovely girl he had seen with the old saint who had so mysteriously reappeared. "Were I Abbas Khan," he thought, "they might cut me in pieces ere I would consent to mate with one like Sukeena, while a girl like the saint's granddaughter was within possibility of attainment. No, it can never be. And what does it matter to Sukeena; her money will attract some one."

"What art thou saying, father?" asked his daughter. "Thy lips move, but no words come forth."

"I was saying," returned her father, bitterly, "that if thou hadst met me with a cheerful face, brought me a pleasant breakfast, and behaved thyself like a loving daughter, I should have patted thee on the head and become more reconciled to thy ugly face. Well! ugly it always was, and that is no fault of thine. Nay, do not cry; but two years have made it sour and forbidding, and all thy wealth would not reconcile it to constant companionship."

Then he got up suddenly, put the girl aside, and went into his bath. I am afraid matters there did not improve the good man's temper. The water had been hastily heated lukewarm, instead of hot; and it had been smoked with the smoke of cowdung cakes till, as the poor Khan said, it would take all the perfumes of a perfumer's shop to take the evil smell from him. He took off his armour, however, and his heavy riding clothes, put on a light muslin suit, went out, and sat down in his accustomed place.

No one was there, but presently his wife appeared, leading a small procession, at the head of which was his daughter bearing a silver plate, and several women with others also covered.

"Spread the cloth," said the Lady Fyzun, "and put down the dishes. Now, Bismilla! Khan Sahib, eat thy fill, for it is consecrated to the Lord," she said with a sniff. "It was about to go forth to the shrine of the Chishtee saint, but I have saved some for thee."

"Bismilla!" he said, as a servant removed a cover, and he expected to find some delicate rice milk or vermicelli, with which he would have been content, hungry as he was; but instead, he saw three "julaybees," very old and leathery, and, moreover, much fly-blown, on the first plate; and on the next, two large coarse "luddoos," which smelt rancid, and were covered with dust, a few very dry hard dates, and two oranges of the peculiarly sour description used by dyers; and on the last, two shrivelled coarse plantains, bruised and black.

"Ul-humd-ul-Illa! Praise be to God!" he exclaimed, "that

my wife and daughter worship the saints, although they need not send them stale sweetmeats and sour and rotten fruits. Do not deny these delicacies to holy men, lady wife; but for me they are much too good, and I must seek plainer food elsewhere," and having delivered this speech with a kind of grave mock solemnity, he took up his sword, tucked it under his arm, and walked away.

"If you are going to Humeed Khan's house to eat," cried his wife, not a whit abashed, "give my humble respects, and say, that when it may be quite convenient, I should like the matter of Sukeena-bee's marriage to be settled."

"Oh, mother!" cried the girl, when her father had departed, "I saw Meeah in the procession to-day, and he is as beautiful as Yoosuf. If I do not marry him I shall die."

I think it is very possible, if Zyn Khan had had a better reception at home, he would have made an attempt to carry this point. As it was, he arrived just as his friend Humeed Khan's cloth was being spread. Nothing was said but a welcome, and the hungry man sat down to a dinner of many savoury courses, which he enjoyed heartily, and felt truly grateful for. And after this, when the three men were alone, and pleasant fumes of fragrant tobacco were being inhaled, they discussed the subject of the marriage in a friendly manner.

"The last words my wife said to me were, that I should settle something about the marriage of your nephew and my daughter;

and as we can talk it over in a friendly manner among ourselves, perhaps we had better make some arrangement."

"Well," said Humeed Khan, "you know it is now a very old matter, with which neither I nor my wife had anything to do; and we have long thought that, as we were not parties to the agreement, and refuse to be so, the issue rests with Meeah alone, who, of course, can claim your daughter if he chooses, and he is now responsible for his own actions. You had better, therefore, ask him, Khan Sahib, and I will withdraw while you discuss it."

"No, no, no!" cried both, "stay with us; and," added Abbas Khan, gravely, "I have fully considered the matter, and have come to the conclusion that it would be better for us both that we continue to be separate."

"And what is to become of Sukeena, Meeah? Is she never to have a husband?"

"She has, or will have, much wealth," replied the young Khan; "and, as flies to honey, so, when it is known that she is free, a hundred suitors will send in their proposals, and you can take your choice. Besides, you are Abyssinians and we are Dekhanies, and such marriages never prosper. Have not a hundred bloody feuds arisen out of such affairs?"

"That is true," said Zyn Khan; "and there is no saying what feud might not arise even at the very marriage itself. All the hot bloods of my people declare that as Meeah slew Elias Khan and his champion, Yacoot, there is a blood feud between the Dekhanies and the Abyssinians which may break out at any time."

"Of course it might," said Humeed Khan; "and of all occasions that of a marriage is the most probable. My friend, not only for our own sakes, but for that of the State, we ought to forbid this matter; and I, for one, shall forbid it, leaving Meeah to pursue his own course."

"Well," returned Zyn Khan, "I can guess what that will be. Sukeena-bee has not grown more beautiful since I left her, and I love you, Meeah, too well, and her too well—for is she not my only child?—to join you together to hate each other all your lives! The old adage, 'Pigeons mate with pigeons, and hawks with hawks,' suits you exactly. My dame can look about for one of our own clan, who are poor enough, but they have the breeding she likes best, and Sukeena will be rich. Now, Humeed Khan, do not be offended if I speak bluntly. My lady is fond of money, and so is Sukeena. Suppose you offer something for the marriage expenses, and I think it will be accepted."

"Good!" cried Humeed Khan, laughing. "I will send five thousand rupees gladly."

"And I," added Abbas Khan, "a pair of gold anklets and a pearl necklace."

"Enough, O generous friends!" cried Zyn Khan. "There

may be some difficulty, perhaps; but, after all, Inshalla! a man is master in his own household."

But when he returned home, Zyn Khan did not find the matter so easy as he had imagined. His daughter declared she should die, and would eat no food. Her mother only pointed to her as she lay, and said, "Let her die, since thou hast not spirit enough to help her." And it was only when the last temptation was offered, the money and the jewels, that mother and daughter seemed to yield before the persistence, not to say obstinacy, of the master of the house.

The affair, however, took nearly a month to arrange, until one day the parties concerned attended at the Kazee's office, in the great Adalut Palace, and mutual deeds of release having been interchanged, Zyn Khan took away with him on his elephant five bags of a thousand rupees each, and the beautiful anklets and pearls which Abbas Khan had presented. The whole had been well managed, without either public scandal or offence to either party. There was nothing in it which was against custom or law, and Abbas Khan was at last free from a connection which he had always dreaded. On the other hand, Sukeena-bee put on her gold anklets and walked about, rejoicing in the music of their tiny bells, and fastened on the necklace, which was declared free from defect; while her mother, for a time very busy among her female friends, at last found out a young man descended from an ancient and noble Abyssinian family, and the betrothment of the pair quickly followed.

"If I had not fasted that day," said the Lady Fyzun, "we should not have secured that happy deliverance from low-bred Dekhanies."

"If I had not taken the affair out of thy hands, O wife, we should have gone on as we were, for Abbas Khan could never have been persuaded."

"Ul-humd-ul-Illa!" ejaculated the husband.

"Ul-humd-ul-Illa!" echoed the dame. "Ameen! Ameen!"

## CHAPTER V.

### CHANGES IN SOME POSITIONS.

FOR some weeks there was no change in the positions of the several characters of our history. The Queen Dowager gradually withdrew herself from public duties, for she found that her nephew, the King, had developed strong talent both for political affairs and internal civil administration. Rewards and dignities had been freely distributed by him; and the troops, satisfied with his liberally granted donations, were serving loyally and steadily throughout the kingdom. There were no rebellions, insurrections, or feuds, nor a spot on the political horizon, from which there was cause for anxiety, except Ahmednugger, whose local affairs were by no means in a settled condition; but with these there was no present or pressing reason to interfere. With his good aunt, King Ibrahim continued on most affectionate terms. Always considered by him as a mother, he resorted to her for advice and counsel in many affairs, of which she had more experience than himself; and as she never displayed the least desire for interference of any kind, the entire harmony between them was never disturbed. The King's fine taste for architecture had full scope in the decoration of his own mausoleum, and the works attached to it, in which Francis d'Almeida and the humble painter often assisted him by suggestions; and with these, and other public undertakings, occasional hunting parties and short excursions, constant durbars and current business, his time was occupied fully and usefully.

Beejapoor was then at its greatest. Owing to the presence of the principal portions of the army, and the cessation of war, trade had increased rapidly, and the general prosperity of the kingdom was as assuring as it was gratifying. Congratulatory letters arrived in due course from Golconda, Beeder, Penkonda, and other kingdoms, accompanied by embassies, which gave rise to many superb entertainments; and, in the words of a local historian, "the songs of revelry and thanksgiving, which the people had not heard for many years, now resounded through the land, and weeping was heard no more."

Zóra's usual life had undergone no alteration. The King would not hear of her grandfather's proposal to change his residence, or to build a house for himself in one of the Royal gardens at Torweh; and indeed, to Zóra's great delight, he made no objection to remaining where he was, under the Royal roof, partaking of the King's hospitality. An additional court, cells, cloisters, and rooms behind them had been set in order for him, and in the enclosure was a small but elegant mosque or chapel for worship, where the old man could give his lectures to many scholars, both in divinity and medicine. He rarely preached in the great Jooma mosque now; the doing so was too great an effort for him, and, on every occasion, the exhaustion which followed was but too evident to all; and Zóra was thankful when, after a more trying sermon than usual, the old man put his hand upon her head, and said, with a sigh, "Child! I can do no more abroad. I will reserve what strength is left to me to teach here."

From that day he went forth no more, except on festival anniversaries, when, attended by his faithful Ahmed—for the Queen now objected to Zóra's appearing in public—he took his place among the worshippers. Even the great Kureem-oo-deen Chishtee was softened, and paid "the saint" many visits, with a display of kindly feeling which was in strong contrast to the bitterness he had once shown.

Zóra had, therefore, more leisure, and there were now other servants to share Ahmed's and Mamoolla's duties. She remained most of her time with the Queen, as has been previously explained, who grew more and more attached to her day by day. Who, indeed, could resist her cheerful, winning disposition, her genial kindliness, and her entire unselfishness and devotion? while every little accomplishment she possessed improved by quiet exercise and study, under one of the Persian secretaries who, in days past, had been the King's, as well as Abbas Khan's, instructor.

She saw little of the Queen, Taj-ool-Nissa. At first, she had been a constant visitor and attendant with Maria, but the Queen was afraid of Zóra's beauty. She knew that in point of manner and of cultivation she was by far inferior to Zóra; and she sent her a kindly message, through Maria, that she must not visit her except on special occasions, when there were entertainments to ladies at which the King could not be present, or when the Dowager Chand Beebee came privately to see her. And the Queen was right. Though her health had improved vastly under the priest's treatment, yet she was still a slight, perhaps insignificant-looking girl —pretty, now that health had given roundness to her form and lustre to her large dreamy eyes; yet she could not be compared for a moment with Zóra, who, with rest, peace, and entire freedom from the anxiety which had hung over her till her innocence was proved before all, was fast attaining her full development of beauty; and it was impossible to compare the now handsomely dressed, well-cared for girl, the beloved companion and attendant of her Royal mistress, with the poorly, coarsely clad and uncared-for girl of the Fakeer's house at Juldroog. Runga Naik, too, had safely transmitted the box of precious articles which had been deposited with him, and in them Zóra found many ornaments which had belonged to her grandmother and her mother, with some garments of cloth of gold, and handsome scarves; but, indeed she hardly needed them, for the kind Queen provided her liberally with all she required; and her grandfather was constantly asking her why she did not buy clothes and jewels, for were they not now rich? But I think the simple, natural tastes of the girl predominated over all love of display or of finery, and she had enough of the latter already.

The Lady Fatima was perhaps more constantly with the Queen than any other lady of the city. They had been intimate friends for years, for the Queen's care of Abbas Khan after his parents' death, and while the Lady Fatima was unavoidably absent, was a strong bond between them. Thus the good lady had many, almost daily, opportunities of seeing Zóra, and observing her disposition in all respects. Her husband and her nephew had enrolled themselves as disciples of the aged Syud, and thus there were already strong bonds of mutual attachment growing up between the families. How well did Fatima Beebee remember Meeah's words in his sleep after the combat; his sweet smile and sigh as he uttered "Zóra! Zóra!" in his dream. Now her husband had seen Zóra. He returned from the durbar of the trial full of Zóra's bravery—her indomitable spirit, and yet of her modesty. "Any other girl," he declared, "would have lost heart, would have sat down and wept, would have flinched from the sore ordeal to which Zóra had been subjected, and out of which she had come forth so triumphantly." Yes, she was satisfied that her nephew had yielded to no unworthy passion, and that his love was as pure as her utmost hope could desire.

When the trial was over, she told what she had heard to her husband, for Abbas Khan had not dared to tell his uncle, while they were in camp, more than of the sad situation of the old Syud, who had been so kind to him, and had left all else to chance, or, as he more reverently expressed himself, to the will of God; and the sudden appearance of the girl by the wayside with her grandfather, as the King passed them, had aroused all the feelings which had been his companions from the night Zóra had watched him till the present. Still, he had said nothing. He knew how deeply he was involved in the old engagement of childhood, which could not be dissolved rudely or suddenly; but the matter should be arranged by the family of Zyn Khan.

After a decent time had passed, and the newly arranged marriage of Sukeena Beebee was proclaimed, and when, in fact, her marriage day was fixed and invitations to it distributed, there was no occasion to delay; and one day, which had been chosen by the family astrologer, the Lady Fatima, urged by her husband, went to the Queen to ascertain whether Zóra loved Abbas Khan, and to ask advice as to how she was to proceed. She did not even mention her intention to her nephew; it would be time enough to speak to him should all be favourable to her design, for she felt certain that his heart had not changed.

Long before the good lady's visit, Queen Chand had discovered as much as she needed to know of the condition of

Zóra's heart. She had hardly entered the audience hall on the day of the King's entry, and taken her seat, than she saw the eyes of Abbas Khan eagerly fixed upon Zóra, and the attempts of Zóra to conceal her face; and during the events of the succeeding day the impression was still more vivid, rising to its fullest height when Abbas Khan accepted the traitor Osman Beg's challenge. Then, indeed, the Queen had read Zóra's heart completely, for her wistful, earnest gaze, which she had no thought to conceal, the flush on her cheek and her now trembling form, betrayed emotions which it was impossible to hide; and from that moment the girl found a place in the Royal heart which filled a long existent yearning. Yet still she never spoke on the subject to Zóra herself. She knew there was a serious obstacle, and whether it could be smoothed away or not seemed very doubtful. But the Queen's mind was more at ease after she knew that Abbas Khan's marriage was broken off. She could not, by reason of her rank, take any steps herself in what she wished; but she was ready at the same time to assist the union of her two children, as she called them, by any and every means in her power.

The Lady Fatima's visit was, therefore, a joyful one to the Queen as soon as she understood its purport; and being a woman of practical mind, she did not use any circumlocution. Would there be any objection on behalf of Zóra's grandfather, or would there be any from the girl herself? Had Her Majesty any other arrangement in view for Zóra, or had the King? These formed the pith of the good lady's communication. To the latter, Queen Chand was enabled to give a decided and favourable answer. Not many days before, the King had said to her laughingly, "It is time, mother, that Abbas Khan was married and settled. Would not Zóra-bee suit him exactly? They are both clever, both handsome, and thou wilt have the most beautiful grandchildren in Beejapoor. For my own part, though I have held my peace, I have been of the same mind ever since Osman Beg's trial; but it is thou as Meeah's mother who should make the first move in the matter; I can but aid thee by giving it my perfect approval."

So, then, the first point was gained. The second was to ascertain whether the parties would be fortunate, and this was decided by the most celebrated astrologer in Beejapoor, who discovered that Abbas Khan was Fire, and Zóra was Air, and the result would be that the utmost degree of love and happiness would reign between them; that Zóra would submit herself to her husband, and that her husband would treat her with great kindness and affection. Such was the decree of the wise man; and then, horoscopes being cast, the result was that a favourable prognostic of the planets occurred in the course of a few days, and it behoved all concerned to make due preparations for the betrothal.

So far the proceedings of the confederates had been eminently successful, and with the dear old Syud there was no difficulty. He had gradually become impressed with the necessity of confiding Zóra to the care of some one whom he could consider worthy of her. In the Queen he knew she had obtained a kind and powerful friend and even motherly care and interest, but that she should be a wife was a higher desire in the old man's mind; but it was coupled to an almost selfish wish that she should not leave him alone. What should he do without her gentle, loving ministrations? How should he find his charms and amulets, or his medicines? Who could read to him or write for him? Who could lead him about, even in the precincts of their present home? Who, in short, could be the companion to him that Zóra was, with her intellect unfolding more and more as weeks passed? He knew no young man but Abbas Khan—Meeah, as he always called him—and his love and respect for him were deep and sincere. But when Abbas Khan went to him with his uncle, and pleaded hard for Zóra, the dear old man grieved bitterly; it seemed as though Zóra were to be taken from him immediately, and he moaned in bitter grief as he rocked himself to and fro in his seat.

"Does Zóra know of this?" he asked. "Does she desire of her own free will to leave me, old and infirm as I am? I will not believe it; I cannot think that she has a hard heart—she who has been so compassionate and so devoted all her life." And it was long ere the young Khan and his uncle could persuade him that she was not to leave him, but that the betrothal would be an assurance to him that Zóra's position would be all that he could desire after the Lord's message should come to him; and so, gradually, he consented, and putting his hands on Meeah's head blessed him and Zóra, who was to be his wife.

And Zóra? She knew nothing of the pleasant plot against her. She had not known even of Abbas Khan's freedom from his former contract, much less of his present intentions; but her love had never changed. From the scenes at Juldroog up to the present time it had grown stronger. No one mentioned Meeah to her except Maria; but why was he ever present in her mind? "Well," she would say to herself, "let it be as the Lord wills!" and so waited the issue. Her grandfather and the Queen were too awful in her estimation to confide in on a subject like this. She dared not mention it to the Lady Fatima; that, indeed, would be like asking for Meeah, and would be bold and immodest; and, for the present, the girl waited quietly and patiently. But her suspense was not to be for long. The day Abbas Khan and his uncle came to her grandfather, the Queen, to whom she was reading, bid her put down the book and come to her; and, wondering, she rose and knelt by her mistress. The suddenness of the request had called up blushes to the lovely face, and the eyes of the girl were cast down. Had she offended in aught?

"No, child," said the Royal lady; "but I have been thinking

it is time thou wert married. Hast thou any preference for any one of the youths thou hast seen or heard of? If thou hast, tell it to me, thy mother. Lay thy head on my breast, and tell it to me. Thou canst trust me, Zora." And she held out her arms.

The child was too truthful to be a coquette, and she could not resist the appeal. Lying in the Queen's arms, and sobbing with excitement, she told all, from the night of the watch to the scene of the trial, and how she thought Meeah would never leave her. "And many have asked Abba to give me away" (and she thought of the Rajah's poor secretary with a smile), "even the great and rich; but I refused, and Abba did not press me. O mother, I love Meeah! I do love him! Is it unmaidenly? Is it wrong? Often I have thought it was, and longed to put on the green dress and take its vows, but Abba always prevented me. Now do as thou wilt with me."

"It is enough, child," returned the Queen, stroking her soft round cheek and kissing her forehead. "Enough for thee, and for those who love thee; and may the Lord bless thee, my darling! I would retire now, and thou wilt go to Abba and Maria." And Zóra rose and went to them. Entering her own apartment, she found Maria there; and, falling on her neck, told her, with many a choking sob, what the Queen had said. Nor was her suspense continued. The Lady Fatima had followed her husband, and being announced, at once opened the subject of her visit. But Zóra could not reply till she had seen her grandfather; and as Humeed Khan and his nephew had departed, and Abba had taken his noonday sleep, there was no one to interrupt them.

I do not think I need follow the scene longer. Under their mutual explanations, and there was no needless reticence, Zóra confessed her love, and was blessed by her grandfather, whom she soothed by the assurance that she would not leave him while he lived. As to the Lady Fatima, she filled Zóra's mouth with sugar-candy, half smothered her in flowers, rubbed her hands, feet, and neck with fragrant paste of sandal-wood; and finally cast over Zóra a rich sheet of brocaded gold tissue, and hung round her neck a costly necklace, as she whispered, "From Meeah." No professional women had been employed, and perhaps they were the only disappointed parties in Beejapoor; but when the pán leaves and spice were distributed from house to house to all the mutual friends of both parties, hearty congratulations followed; and even the female gossips of the city—who, as elsewhere, were very numerous—were satisfied that it was a good match.

There are nearly as many ceremonies to complete a Mussulman betrothal as there are in a marriage; but I do not think my readers, even my lady readers, would care to follow them through perhaps two whole chapters, and will rest content in being assured that Zóra's happiness and state in life have been secured as far as human foresight could provide, and that there were no more hearty or more loving wishes for her than those of Sister Maria and her brother Francis. We, therefore, can leave our old friends the Syud and Zóra, now familiar with new positions and new hopes, full of contentment and joyful anticipation to both—more especially to Zóra, whose mingled feelings of love, gratitude, and faith could perhaps have been hardly definable.

Among the various letters of congratulation which reached the King Ibrahim was one from the Viceroy and Captain-General of Goa, Dom Matthias de Abuquerque, which—with a valuable present of various kinds of arms, European manufactures, and valuables—was brought by a special ambassador, the Captain Don Miguel de Gama, an officer of respectability and consideration, well acquainted with the Persian language, and therefore most fitting for an ambassador. The ambassador's suite was not numerous; but as he rode into the city early one morning in a full panoply of bright steel armour, and presented his credentials at the public durbar in the same equipment, he created no little excitement. The captain, too, was of a noble, commanding presence, and had fought well against the Moors in many battles; and this specimen of the local chivalry of Goa was in every degree a good representative of its renown.

The letter was in Portuguese, and could have been translated by the ambassador himself, but the King decided that our friend Francis D'Almeida should act as secretary and interpreter; and at the early durbar of the morning, after the ambassador's arrival, the worthy captain, in no degree abashed by the splendour around him, marched up the great hall, his armour clanking as he moved, and saluting King Ibrahim gracefully, laid his packet of letters at the King's feet.

The captain had come direct to the house of the painter, and had been comfortably lodged. And how much had Francis and his sister to hear of their friends at Goa, of the proceedings of Dom Diego, and of the innumerable changes in the local society; but withal, there was the certainty that they would have to return to Goa, whether in his company or apart, to answer the charges which had been preferred against them by Dom Diego in the inquisition.

And when the Viceroy's letter was read aloud by the priest, after congratulations upon peace and prosperity of Beejapoor since the detection and destruction of the conspiracy and insurrection of the Prince Ismail, a passage followed which related to Francis D'Almeida and his sister, which may be quoted:—"And furthermore, it hath been represented to us that a certain priest, Francis D'Almeida, and his sister Doña Maria, were detected in intrigues with the rebels, and received from them sundry large sums of money for the supply of European troops and cannon, which would have been an act beyond the bounds of good-will and peace between us, and for which they have, very justly, been detained by the Government of our friend and ally, yet, as subjects of the kingdom of Portugal, and as Francis D'Almeida and his sister belong to religious orders of the Church of Christ, they should be permitted to answer the charges that have been made against them; and we, in the name of the King, our master, request that they may be sent to us in company with our envoy."

When they returned home, Francis learned from his sister that she had heard all from the Queen's balcony. She was weeping, but was not cast down. "I knew it would come upon us sooner or later. The Church never sleeps, and we cannot delay compliance with this order;" for a fresh citation had been delivered to them requiring instant obedience. "We must go, brother, even to the stake, if it be the Lord's will."

"I fear not, Maria. I have always thought from the first that it would have been best to go to Goa; and yet the inscrutable ways of Providence who can follow? Should we have discovered Dom Diego's letters to Osman Beg or Elias Khan, which on the political charge will acquit us? As for the rest, conscious as we are of innocence, I fear nothing. Those, too"—and he pointed to the translations he had made in company with the Brahmins of the old college in the fort—"will prove that I have not been lax in my work, though we have been here. No, sister, let us go. I am to attend the night council, and the King's reply to the Viceroy will be drafted."

And it was all the good priest could have wished for. The King, the Queen Dowager, Kureem-oo-deen Chishtee, Ekhlas Khan, the Kazee, and some others, discussed every point of the Portuguese letter, in the ambassador's presence (who, divested of his armour, and dressed in a suit of black Genoa velvet, looked, as he was truly, a courtly gentleman), and every incident that had occurred at Beejapoor was detailed. At first the priest of Moodgul had been under suspicion; but that had passed away owing to the discovery of the treachery of Dom Diego, and he was left to be dealt with by the laws of Portugal; but the money he had obtained from Beejapoor subjects ought to be restored.

The Queen Dowager and the King's wife, as well as Zóra and the good Lady Fatima, were sincerely grieved by the necessity of the absence of their friends, and the old Syud, Meeah and his uncle, no less so. "I shall see thee no more, O friend," said the Syud, grasping the priest's hand. "Christian and Moslem we have lived together in amity, and I am thankful. If God will, and thou return hither, we may meet again; if not, the blessing of Allah be with thee and thine."

And Maria, though her fortitude and her faith supported her in the trial, yet was sorely pained to leave her friends. Taj-ool-

Nissa, who had become deeply attached to her, and also Zóra, were in despair; but Maria had her own sources of comfort which never failed her, and a few days after, with the tears and blessings of all, she and her brother, well provided with palanquins and tents, and under the charge of an officer of the Court, who spoke Portuguese, though after a rude fashion, departed from the Royal city in eace.

## CHAPTER VI.

### PROCEEDINGS AT GOA.

It was now the beginning of October, and the rains had ceased; all but those occasional slight showers which lend freshness to the air, maintain the verdure of the later crops of grain, and furnish those magnificent sunsets which form the glory of the month. Supplied with comfortable palanquins, and well provided with horses from the Royal stables, Maria, her brother, and their friend the envoy, often rode together in the cool morning air; and Maria enjoyed heartily the healthful exercise to which, in the crowded city of Beejapoor, she had long been a stranger.

And thus they sped on from day to day, accompanied by old Pedro and his wife, who were overjoyed at quitting the great city of the Moors, and beholding once more their beautiful and beloved Goa. On the plateau above the Ghâts the scenery had been tame and monotonous; fine undulating plains covered with luxuriant crops of grain and cotton presented little for admiration or for interest; but near the crest, heavy forests and broken peaks of mountains furnished beautiful combinations of wild scenery, and the view over the broad districts of the Concan was inexpressibly lovely. Away in the west, the sea stretched to the dim horizon, and here and there the tiny white speck of a sail could be distinctly seen. Nearer, however, a dense white mist filled all the valleys and covered the plain, until the sun, just rising, fell upon it, causing it to glitter like a sea of molten silver, with occasional rugged peaks rising out of it like islands. Then all seemed to break up; and while some of the mist clung to the sides of the greater elevations, the rest gradually rose into the air and disappeared.

From the last stage the captain envoy left them to give notice of their arrival. He would fain have taken the King's letter with him, and the presents by which it was accompanied, which consisted of vessels inlaid with silver and gold, cloths of gold and silver, four fine Dekhan horses, and an elephant; but Francis d'Almeida claimed the privilege of presenting these himself, especially as they were accompanied by Dom Diego's letters, and he was doubtful as to what use or misuse might be made of them. He sent, however, by the captain a letter to the head of the order to which he belonged, and Doña Maria another to the Lady Abbess of the convent of which she was a lay sister; and on their arrival in the city, Francis consigned his sister to the care of the Abbess, who received her with warm affection, for she had been now several years absent, and she felt in a short time at rest and at ease among many of her old friends and associates. In like manner Francis took up his residence in his old quarters; and it seemed to him that nothing had changed there, and that all was as peaceful as when he had left it several years before his sister's arrival.

But within the religious society of Goa there was not peace. There were strivings between the orders, which the Archbishop strove to reconcile; and the present Viceroy, Don Matthias de Gama, a kind, benevolent man in the main, and an excellent and brave soldier, found it difficult at times to control all and keep up his own authority. Since Dom Diego's arrival, contention had increased. The Archbishop had been appealed to by the Superior of the Jesuits, to demand the surrender of Francis d'Almeida and his sister as contumacious heretics. Nothing less than their trial and execution would, he declared, satisfy the demands of the Holy Church, and preserve discipline in the distant Churches over which only a very partial supervision could be exercised. Dom Diego preached several public sermons in the Church of his order, in which the apostasy of Francis, and his sorceries and evil consorting with heathens and Moors, were set forth with violent eloquence; and these excited his hearers to a powerful degree, so that even in the Church they cried out, "Death to the wretch! Death to the apostate!"

On the other hand, the Archbishop, who well knew Francis

d'Almeida's value as a missionary, his power of language in addressing the heathen, his knowledge of native dialects, and the practical use of his translations and ministerial offices, defended him, and there were many others who followed his example. In process of these disputes, the Viceroy was appealed to, who declared that the case was one of ecclesiastical interest only; and though he was bound to assist the Church, yet the parties accused were beyond his jurisdiction, residing, or perhaps prisoners, in a powerful kingdom, with which Portugal was at peace; and, moreover, that in regard to the allegations against the priest and his sister, the Church itself was by no means unanimous in opinion. He declined, therefore, to take any steps in regard to them. If they were contumacious it was no affair of his. The Church could excommunicate them if it pleased. At last, however, yielding to pressure, the Viceroy had written, as we know. The Viceroy had sent a complimentary letter to the King of Beejapoor, despatched it by a trustworthy soldier, and awaited the issue with considerable interest as to whether the accused persons would in reality make submission and appear, or whether, becoming renegades, as many had done, they would altogether defy the Church and become Moors. But the arrival of Francis and his sister, escorted by a Beejapoor officer and a guard of the King's troops, was proof to all that no contumacy was intended; and he appointed an early Council, at which the Beejapoor letter should be read, and necessary consideration made of the whole of the circumstances.

A few days afterwards the Beejapoor envoy and Francis d'Almeida received their summons from the Viceroy to attend his Council and the Court, and they went together, the envoy being attended by his escort, which, in their suits of chain mail and rich apparel, made an imposing appearance in the thronged streets of the city; and on their arrival at the palace were ushered at once into the presence of the Viceroy, who, with his staff about him, was seated on the viceregal throne.

An artillery salute was fired in honour of the envoy, who was graciously received; and after some general and kind inquiries after the health of King Ibrahim, to which he replied in indifferent Portuguese, the rest of the conversation was carried on through Francis d'Almeida, who acted as interpreter. Then the Viceroy, receiving the King's letter, said, "As this contains matter for political consideration, we will adjourn, Sir Envoy, to our Council Hall, where it shall be read before all my councillors of State and dignitaries of the Church, who are our advisers." Then, rising and taking the envoy's hand, he led him into the adjoining apartment, which was the Council Chamber.

It was a fine room, though to the envoy's idea somewhat bare of decoration. A large Turkey carpet was laid upon the floor, and in the centre was a long table covered with red cloth, with inkstands and writing paper ready for use. The Viceroy seated himself at the head of the table, placed the envoy in a chair on his right hand, and the dignitaries of the Church, military and naval commanders, all wearing their rich uniforms and decorations, took their seats with the civil officers, according to precedence and custom. The whole formed a dignified and, indeed, august assembly, well befitting the powerful kingdom it represented.

Then the letter of King Ibrahim was read, and the Viceroy remarked that it was written in excellent Portuguese, and asked his envoy to Beejapoor who wrote it, and the captain said—

"In my presence was it written by the priest Francis d'Almeida. The King himself dictated the letter in Persian, in my presence, and the purport was fully known to me; and the priest and I compared the Portuguese version with the Persian, and they corresponded exactly. Moreover, your Excellency will observe that the original Persian is written below, and signed by the King himself. There can be no doubt of the authenticity of both."

"But," continued the Viceroy, "in the latter portion of this document grave charges are made against Dom Diego di Fonseca, an eminent servant of the Church, who is now the accuser of Francis d'Almeida and his sister Maria, and at whose instance, and that of the Holy Father of the Inquisition, their presence was required in order to answer the charges brought against them, and we ought not to enter into this subject without his presence. As it is a political affair entirely, involving the risk of disagreement between our Government and that of our friend King Ibrahim the Second, we, the representatives of Portugal, have full authority to investigate it, leaving the alleged offenders against the Church to be dealt with by the Holy Inquisition. Let, therefore, Dom Diego be summoned instantly; and till he arrives we call upon Francis d'Almeida to give an account of his apparent flight from Moodgul, and his evasion of the summons of the Inquisition."

"I was not a free agent, may it please your Excellency and the members of this Council," said Francis d'Almeida. "I was preparing to leave Moodgul after the citation was publicly read by my colleague when I was arrested, by order of the Queen Regent of Beejapoor, and forwarded by Dilawar Khan, the Governor of Moodgul, to the fort of Juldroog, where we were confined for more than a month on charges of having conspired against the State in assisting the conspiracy of the Prince Ismail and Eyn-ool-Moolk, and obtaining large sums of money for the purpose of engaging European soldiers and cannon. Finally, we were sent to Beejapoor, where we remained under surveillance until the King should return, as the Queen Regent did not consider she had authority to try so momentous a question herself. Then suddenly, and as by special Providence, certain papers fell into the hands of the Queen's Government, by which it appeared that my colleague, and not I, had been in correspondence with the rebels, partly independently, and partly by means of Osman Beg, the Killadar or Governor of the fort of Juldroog, who was arrested, tried on the evidence of papers found in his possession, convicted of treason, and sentenced to death."

"And he was beheaded, Francis d'Almeida?" asked the Viceroy.

"Not so, my lord; his life was spared on the intercession of his cousin, Abbas Khan; but he was banished from the kingdom, and has taken his departure for Mecca with his father."

Francis d'Almeida's address had continued for some time, for he described minutely and concisely all that had occurred, with the particulars of which we are fully acquainted.

"And where are the papers you allude to?" asked the Superior of the Inquisition tartly. "Who can vouch for their authenticity if they are produced?"

"My lord," returned the Beejapoor envoy, "we are not careless in regard to papers of importance at Beejapoor. At the first discovery of them, after the death of Yacoot, the Abyssinian, I, as knowing somewhat of your language, was asked to read those in Portuguese; but I could not, and the Padré Sahib was directed by the Queen to do so, and to translate them into Persian; then her seal was affixed to each one of them, and she added her private signature, and all the Ministers signed and sealed them. Then the packet was sealed until opened by order of the King, and sealed again with his seal, which all men know, and which is appended to his letter."

"You were all very careful," said the chief Inquisitor, with a sneer, "but where are these letters?"

At this moment Dom Diego was ushered in. He wore the religious dress of his order, but he at once threw back his cowl, and his eyes and those of Francis d'Almeida met once more. In the one was a scowl of bitter hate, and the brows were almost knit together; but those of Francis wore their usual mild expression, and betrayed no emotion; nay, their look of innocence seemed to make a favourable impression upon all present.

After bending his knee to the Archbishop and the Grand Inquisitor, Dom Diego drew his fine figure to its full height, looked round the room towards all, and then said to the Viceroy, "For what purpose am I required here, most illustrious Sir? I have not been apprised that matters which are under the cognisance of the Holy Inquisition could be transferred to a Council like this; and I request that my protest may be entered against any interference with what has been already arranged."

"There is no intention, Dom Diego, on our part to interfere with the proceedings of the Holy Office. This is a political question, which thou wilt know of when thou hast heard the letter of the King of Beejapoor. Let it be read to him," he continued, "as also the minutes of Francis d'Almeida's statement."

Dom Diego heard all without reply; but it was easy to see that his mind was far from tranquil. A nervous tremor appeared to be irrepressible; his mouth twitched as if by convulsion, and he twisted his hands together in continuous action, which could be seen even under his robe.

"And now, my lords," said the Viceroy, rising, "the most important part of our sitting is to commence; and I have to beg, in the name of justice, that your utmost vigilance may be employed to clear up what has been alleged. The papers alluded to in the letter are in possession of the envoy from Beejapoor. Let him produce them."

"They are here, my lord," returned the envoy, producing two small bundles tied up in waxed cloth, which was sealed with the King's seal. "First, I ask you to bear me witness that these seals are intact; and particularly you, O most illustrious Sir, into whose hands I commit the packets."

The Viceroy examined the papers carefully, and said, "I see no reason to doubt what has been said. The seals are undisturbed; but judge for yourselves, noble sirs." And when the packets had passed round, the Viceroy demanded to know whether they were to be accepted, and a general reply was given that they were.

"These are the letters which were found on the body of Yacoot, the Abyssinian. Let them be first examined," said the Beejapoor envoy; "and my lords will please to remark that all have the Queen's seal, as those first found were examined by her; and that there are forty-two documents which, with the exception of those required by the Council, should be returned to me, and a receipt given to me for the remainder. And now, noble sirs, have I your permission to open the first packet?"

"I again protest," cried Dom Diego, rising suddenly, "against any examination of those papers here. Let them be given over to the custody of the Holy Office, which will examine and authenticate them, and produce such as it considers necessary for the elucidation of the truth."

But the pretence was too shallow to escape the detection of many of the experienced men who heard the protest, and the majority at once declared that they should be opened, and publicly read and registered.

Then the Viceroy took the first packet and handed it to his own interpreter, a fine-looking Mussulman gentleman, who had just entered the room, and who spoke not only Arabic and Persian fluently, but Portuguese, for he had lived for some years in Portugal, acting as interpreter of documents sent by the Indian Government. Abdoolla-bin-Ali was a man held by everyone in the highest esteem and honour, and his presence carried assurance with it to all the Council, and very especially to the Beejapoor envoy and Francis d'Almeida, whose personal explanations would be needed no longer.

"On the cover is written," said the Moonshee, "'This packet contains forty-two documents, eighteen in Portuguese and twenty-four in Persian, and bears the King's seal.'" Then he broke the seal carefully and unwound the silken cord with which the parcel was fastened. There appeared within several other coverings, two separate packets, one of which was labelled in Persian, "Eighteen Portuguese papers and letters," and bore the Queen's seal, which was shown to all.

"I think, my lords," said the Viceroy, "that to prevent doubt I had better read these aloud to the Council, and they can examine each separately afterwards, if they please;" and, this being assented to, he took up the first, which was addressed to the most illustrious the Vizier Eyn-ool-Moolk, Bahadoor, and dated from Moodgul. As the letter was opened, everyone could see the strong bold characters of the hand-writing of Dom Diego, which were known to all or most present, and a general murmur ran through the Council, as if of wonder and astonishment; but no one spoke, and, in breathless silence, the Viceroy read on.

It was a long letter, and we may be pardoned for not following it in detail; but the writer acknowledged the receipt of Eyn-ool-

Moolk's "letter offering the Padré Dom Diego de Fonseca a command in the new Royal army. That if he joined it with a force of one thousand Europeans, his pay would be at the rate of one lakh of rupees per month, and the same for every thousand more brought to the Royal standard." It then proceeded to state, that considering the expense of European troops in the field, the pay would be insufficient; and that, in case of the force capturing Beejapoor, there was no mention of prize shares in the treasure and jewels that would become the property of the army. It would be necessary also to confer upon the writer the district of Bunkapoor, with all its forts and dependencies. That as the cowardly and imbecile Government of Goa would never be induced to take part in the war, or to send any of its soldiers, the writer must be provided with funds to go to Portugal to raise as many men as possible, with whom he pledged himself to return at the expiration of a year, and disembark them at any port on the coast that might be chosen.

In conclusion, the writer professed his high admiration for and sympathy with, the movement to substitute the virtuous Prince Ismail for the tyrant who now ruled over Beejapoor, and ended by praying that the measure might receive the blessing and guidance of the Almighty; and at the end was written,

"By mine own hand,

"D. DIEGO DI FONSECA."

"Are there more like that?" asked the Grand Inquisitor of Dom Diego, in a whisper; "if so, thou art lost!"

"Let them read what they will," he answered. "I will satisfy my lord presently."

More! yes, there was much more. Every one of the letters contained sketches of arrangements to be made, estimates of cost, professions of good faith and sincerity. Several of them contained receipts for large sums of money, partly in gold, partly in bills; and by his own admissions Dom Diego had received upwards of three lakhs of rupees in cash, while assurances of payment as far as ten lakhs, beside a fourth share of the plunder of Beeja-poor, was promised and accepted.

Then followed letters to Elias Khan, as the lieutenant-in-chief of Eyn-ool-Moolk, which were in a more familiar strain; which spoke of revelries they had enjoyed together; of the pleasures they would share when they met again; complained that he could not absent himself without suspicion, but that he was about to rid himself of his coadjutor, whose sister Maria he would bring with him, a lovely girl of his own country, who would put to shame all the dusky beauties of his friend's harem; and wine from Portugal of the choicest kind, which should enliven them. In another, the gold sent by the company under Pedro di Diaz, that is, twenty thousand "hoons," had arrived safely; with many other details, all written in the same bold hand, and signed with the same very remarkable signature. As they were read, minutes were made of them by the secretary. Every paper was compared as to the seals of the Queen Regent and the Beejapoor Ministers, and that every precaution had been used to prevent any chance of their being tampered with, was a fact which was not without significance in the assembly.

And the Persian letters to Elias Khan from Eyn-ool-Moolk, with one from the Prince Ismail, bestowing an honorary title as commander of five thousand in the Royal army, with an estate of twenty villages in the district of Bunkapoor—all confirmed the tenor of the Portuguese letters of Dom Diego; while, with the transmission of money through Elias Khan, assurance was given that as soon as the Europeans appeared in the field, the whole of the Talooq of Bunkapoor would be made over to him as stipulated. There were others from Osman Beg to Elias Khan, descriptive of private revels at Moodgul, in a house in the town hard by the Padré, where wine of the choicest was stored up, and was plentiful, and the most beautiful dancing women of the country round were assembled. And he wrote of the Padré as being a jovial fellow, who winked at everything, and who had shown him at the chapel, privately, the beautiful Doña Maria, whom he was to bring away with him when he came with his troops. "She is more lovely than anything on the earth's face, and no Houri of Paradise could be more beautiful;" and much more to the same effect, written in the loose, not to say indecent, style prevailing among those like Osman Beg at Beejapoor. Then the letters seemed suddenly to come to an abrupt close. After May of that year none had passed between the parties; and, indeed, by this time, the whole conspiracy had collapsed in the defeat and deaths of the principal conspirators. There only remained the exposure of the guilt of all by the discovery of the letter on the person of the Abyssinian.

The second packet contained, for the most part, letters from Eyn-ool-Moolk to Elias Khan; but they gave particulars of the agreement with the illustrious and learned Padré D. Diego di Fonseca; of the moneys transmitted to be paid to him; and in one, the Padré's receipt, in Persian and Portuguese, of the twenty thousand hoons, and for other sums, amounting to about two lakhs of rupees.

"Hast thou nothing to reply, brother?" said the Inquisitor, in an earnest whisper to Dom Diego. "Thou art condemned by thine own hand; would it had been cut off and burnt before those letters were written."

Diego did not reply. He rose, and those who were watching him saw that his lips were white, and his dark complexion had assumed an ashy hue, and that he spoke as if he were choked by thirst. Yet he drew himself up bravely, and said with an assumed air of unconcern and bravado, "I am not on my trial, most illustrious Señor, else my reply would be sharp and certain. In these letters, which purport to be mine, I only see the cunning toils with which Francis d'Almeida strove to entangle me, and failed; and when they had nothing to fall back upon they fled. Their being arrested is a mere mockery. As to the handwriting of the letters," and he took up one before the Inquisitor, "they are all like this, forgeries. The fair Maria is an accomplished scribe, and can copy any style of writing, even that of heathen characters; and I do not at all marvel at her excellent imitation of mine. But, my lords, as I said, I am not on my trial; and no opinion can be given on the subject either till I am, or till that shameless priest and his sister are pronounced guilty of heresy and conspiracy by the Holy Inquisition, and perish for their heresies at the stake."

"Let that be as the good God wills," said the Viceroy, calmly. "Meanwhile, these papers are so strong against thee, that we, in virtue of our authority, declare thee to be a prisoner, and arrest thee in the name of our gracious King. Thou shalt have honourable treatment as a gentleman, and thou shalt be lodged in this palace, till the time when the trial of Francis d'Almeida and his sister comes on. When may it be, Holy Father?"

"It is fixed for Friday," answered the Inquisitor, calmly; "that the guilty may be ready for the *auto-da-fé* on the Sabbath. But your Excellency, pardon me, errs in keeping a son of the Church in arrest till then, and I will gladly be security for his appearance when needed."

"Impossible," replied Don Matthias de Gama. "Nevertheless I will take the votes of the Council." And he did so; but none supported the Grand Inquisitor's proposal except one, another priest, and Dom Diego was consigned to the care of the men-at-arms, who conducted him to an upper chamber luxuriously furnished, and told him that his servants would be sent when they could be found to attend to his comfort.

What were the thoughts of this man as he heard the door of his arge airy apartment locked after him and bolted outside. All his reliance on the comparative insignificance of Francis d'Almeida had given place to a fearful sense of his power with hose terrible documents in his own handwriting to appeal to. Forgeries! who would believe that, with all the evidence of his handwriting in the Holy Office, and the Archbishop's records to appeal to for comparison? His accusation against Francis and his sister had depended for success upon his words only, which he believed would overwhelm those of the modest, unassuming priest; and in the death of him and of his sister would be future safety. But the revelation of his own conduct, of the moneys he had obtained, of his treasonable plots, denounced by the King Ibrahim, had rendered his malignity abortive. And now the grim trial, the horrible torture, the death by fire, like that he had witnessed of hapless victims writhing in agony at the stake——

Escape! was it possible? He went to one of the windows and looked through the jalousies, for he could not open one of them. Impossible! his room was over fifty feet from the ground, and the wall was smooth, without a projection; and he turned away with a shudder.

Presently his servant came. "Have you seen Pedro di Diaz?" he asked.

"I have, Señor," was the reply; "and he is now waiting for me at the quay. He wants to know whether he is to stand out to sea or remain."

"Tell him," replied Dom Diego, "that he is to leave the ship's boat with six of the best of the men in it, and to take the brigantine to the mouth of the harbour, without exciting suspicion. I will be with him on Friday night; but if I do not come by Sunday, I shall be dead."

## CHAPTER VII.

### THE INQUISITION.

THE appointed day arrived. The sudden arrest of Dom Diego, his confinement to the Viceregal palace, and the refusal of the Grand Inquisitor's security for him, had created a sensation in Goa which had only one chance of solution—the trial by the Inquisition. On the other hand, the well-known character of Francis d'Almeida, and the devotion of his lovely sister, gave to the case an interest such as had been rarely felt, and never exceeded, in the city. All had many personal friends, Dom Diego especially among the Jesuits, to whose order he belonged; Francis d'Almeida among those of his own order, the Dominicans, and among the ordinary clergy of the province, headed by the noble Archbishop; and in his sweet sister every lady in Goa was interested. Could so holy and learned a woman be actually tried on charges of sorcery and conspiracy with Moors and heathens? And yet it was to be; and many thought that the interference by the Viceroy with the acts of the Holy Office was at once presumptuous and wicked. From early morning the principal street of the city and the square of the Inquisition had been thronged with eager inquirers, and the most conflicting rumours were prevalent; some, that Dom Diego had confessed his guilt, and would be made over to the Inquisition, to be formally condemned; others, that Francis d'Almeida and his sister had made similar confessions, and that all parties had been originally bound in one confederation, but had split upon the division of money of which they had become possessed. In short, the wildest rumours prevailed, particularly as to the sorceries of d'Almeida and his sister, which they had learned from heathen priests and exercised upon their coadjutor to drive him away from the place he had usurped. All these opinions, however, were set at rest by the appearance of two processions: one, that of soldiers of the Viceroy having Dom Diego in their charge; the other of monks and holy nuns, who escorted Francis d'Almeida and his beautiful sister. Among the soldiers Dom Diego marched firmly and proudly, his tall, martial figure being conspicuous from his general bearing, and the haughty manner with which he regarded the crowds who gazed upon him; the others, from the apparent simplicity of the brother and sister, who walked hand in hand, with a calm and submissive demeanour which deeply affected many. No one dared to speak, but whispered comments passed among the crowd; and women, and men too, wept that such servants of God might be condemned ere the day passed, not only to torture, but to the horrible death by fire in the *auto-da-fé* of the next Sabbath, which promised to be one of unusual interest.

So, passing on, both parties entered the portal of the great gloomy building, Dom Diego being the first. And when a short colloquy had passed between the officers of the Viceroy's guard and those of the Inquisition as to the delivery of the prisoner, he was taken on by the familiars. Before the monks and sisters, with the two others, had entered the gate, they had recommenced a hymn which had been sung at intervals during their progress, the sweetness and solemnity of which had had a profound effect; and it again arose steadily and sweetly, with a rich and fervent melody which penetrated every heart, as knees were bent and hats doffed reverently as the processions passed, while the simple words caused many a silent prayer to arise to the Throne of Grace.

When in trouble and in fear,
To thee we cry, O Mother dear!
Behold our sorrows, bitter weeping,
Yet in all trial humbly keeping
Trust in thee, Maria!

Mother of Jesus, lowly born,
On earth by human sorrow torn;
Yet in thy glory resting now,
Heedful of all thy creatures' woe,
Hear our prayer, Maria!

Those who have daily died the death
Of those who suffer slander's breath;
Those who in dread judgment's hour
Their simple hearts to thee outpour,
Pity them, O Maria!

Support them in their hour of need,
To cheer them with thy comfort speed,
Lest without thee they go astray,
Mother, with thee all bright their way,
Having no fear, Maria!

While the chant proceeded, the procession entered the door, and its sweet melody was heard faintly as it passed up the broad corridor which led to the great hall of the Inquisition.

It was a bare, whitewashed room, with narrow windows near the ceiling, which let in the cool air and a small degree of light; but when the eye, dazzled by the glare without, had become accustomed to the dimness within, everything—nay, even the emotions in every face—were distinctly visible. There was a separate place for the accuser; another for the prisoners; and a third for any witnesses that might have to be called. In the centre was a long narrow table covered with coarse black serge, with inkstands, pens, and paper at intervals; and the Inquisitors sat in tall, straight-backed, wooden chairs around, the Grand Inquisitor's position being in the centre of the right hand side, in a raised chair, so that he could overlook all. There were no guards near Dom Diego now; and his cowl being thrown back, his grim, swarthy features and bold flashing eyes were distinctly visible. The prisoners were directed to stand in their allotted space; and the venerable Archbishop, in his robes, with a number of clergy, sat on one side, but took no part in the inquiry.

After the proceedings had been opened by a prayer and a solemn chant, the Grand Inquisitor rose from his seat, and said—

"Holy fathers, we have heard with unfeigned sorrow, grief, and amazement the scandal to the Church which has arisen under the unseemly contentions in the Mission Church at Moodgul, where, in the midst of Moors and Pagans, the Lord Christ hath graciously hitherto supported our poor measures for making known His gospel to those otherwise benighted and damnable peoples. In process of years many hundreds have been gathered to the foot of the Cross, and hundreds have died in a steady belief in the sacraments of the Holy Church, while many live in the exercise of a devout Christian faith and good works. Within the last few months, however, grievous troubles have arisen, as is known to our Father in God the illustrious Archbishop; and on the direct accusations of Dom Diego di Fonseca, the local vicar, we summoned Francis d'Almeida and his sister Maria to answer his charges. This citation was publicly made known to them both by being read in the Mission Church; but, instead of obeying it, both departed from Moodgul under the escort of Moorish soldiers, and went or were conveyed to Beejapoor, where they resided until a demand from His Excellency the Viceroy was made for them, and they were sent hither.

"Thus, holy fathers, ye have to determine in what manner the priest Francis d'Almeida is guilty, as also his sister, of the formal charges which I now read. Then you will hear the justification of the prisoners; and you will, with prayer to the Almighty, pronounce judgment upon them. Diego di Fonseca, in the name of the Holy Trinity, I call upon you to swear that what you are about to say is true;" and on the formal oath being administered to him, he stood erect, and with all the energy and musical tone of his fine voice, he spoke to the following effect.

I think, however, that I do right in refusing an attempt to detail all. In the outset of his oration, he referred to his services in China, in the Spice Islands, in Bengal, among the savage tribes of Malays and Moors; of perils by land and sea, and of the many human souls he had rescued from everlasting destruction.

"I was a humble follower of St. Francis Xavier," he continued, "and strove to follow his example. Then, worn out and weary, I came to Goa, and would have returned to Portugal for a season, but new work at Moodgul was opened to me, and in my zeal I accepted it.

"Holy fathers, when I arrived there I found a mockery of a Church. My coadjutor, more a heathen than a Christian, had suffered the most ordinary offices of the Church to be utterly neglected. He was incessantly employed in the study of Pagan languages, mythology, and Scripture, and of Moorish languages, and infidel books. To the people he invariably preached in a tongue they call Canarese. He read the services of the Church in the same tongue, and he desecrated the holy service by using it even in the mass. Instead of our own language, his sister taught it in the schools, and thus perverted the minds of children, who might have been made wise unto salvation.

"It was all horrible! horrible! this perpetual study of books, which contain besides damnable theological dissertations; works on sorcery, divination, astrology, and all the evil sciences denounced by the Church, for which so many have suffered; and I warned him on many occasions, for I was willing to save them both, to abandon these evil courses and damnable heresies. And at first Francis d'Almeida strove to justify himself by declaring that he read Hindoo books to understand best how to controvert their doctrine; and declared that he was even translating the holy gospels and services of the Church into the language of the people, that they might understand what they profess to believe. Was any heresy ever so complete? Ye, O reverend fathers, know how the Scriptures are forbidden to be read except under ghostly direction and counsel, and how corruption and unbelief must needs arise under such proceedings as those of Francis d'Almeida towards his ignorant flock I found remonstrance of no use; he avoided me with disrespect; and in the congregation a party was growing up against him which it was impossible for me to overcome; I therefore complained to the most reverend the

Archbishop and the Holy Office, and a citation to Francis d'Almeida was sent.

"Meanwhile a strange numbness of mind was stealing over me. I never saw Doña Maria without trembling and confusion. I could not pray; I could not think. I could not even eat; and I knew that her satanic influence was exerted after the heathen manner, to lead me to perdition. But from this I was mercifully preserved. On the day I delivered the citation, she and her brother left their house at night and took refuge with the Moorish Governor, who at once sent them to Juldroog, and thence they were taken to Beejapoor. I was then free; a great weight seemed to be removed from me, and I came hither to lay all before the Church and seek ghostly counsel. Fathers, my short statement is ended; but of heresy and sorcery of the most devilish kind I accuse them both, and demand that in consonance with the laws of the Holy Office they suffer death by fire, and that thus the Church be purged from their spiritual uncleanness. I could extend this address to a vast length, but it would needlessly occupy time. The books in Francis d'Almcida's and his sister's handwriting will satisfy you of the character of their work, and I have brought such as I could find; the rest were concealed before their departure."

"Have you any witnesses to the truth of the accusation?" asked the Grand Inquisitor.

"I have none," he replied, "but God, and one of the deacons who accompanied me, who has charge of the books. How was I to confide to anyone the misery I endured?"

"Dost thou object to these being produced, Francis d'Almeida?"

"No," he said, mildly. "If they are in my own or my sister's writing, they are homilies of the Church, the Vulgate as allowed to the people even here in Goa, and some extracts from the Scriptures such as are given to children."

"Look at these," said the Archbishop. "Are these the same as thou sentest to us for approval?"

D'Almeida opened the books one by one, and looked over the contents. "These are the rough drafts in my own handwriting of the translations as I made them, and here and there I find a small portion of my sister's manuscript. These are the drafts from which she made the fair copies, which in her beautiful characters and ornamented with initial letters are now at Moodgul, in the keeping of one Ramana and other deacons of the mission, and have the illustrious Archbishop's imprimatur on them."

"Yes," said the Prelate and the Grand Inquisitor, "for we had them checked by the Fra Don Francisco da Pinto, who was the best scholar then in Goa. He is now in Madagascar; but, if I remember right, we all signed them."

"They are here, fathers," cried a venerable old man, with long white hair streaming over his shoulders, who, with several others, now made their way into the room, and prostrated themselves on the floor. "Listen to our cry for justice! When our beloved Padré was threatened, and when the pure Señora Maria was insulted, and the Governor of Moodgul sent them away as prisoners, the books were given to us, and we hid them; but when the great Padré was going to Goa, to accuse our beloved friends, I and these with me followed him, and we arrived this morning, O holy fathers, that we may be in time yet to speak the truth before ye! Day and night we have travelled, and we have had no fear save of delay."

"And who are ye?" asked the Grand Inquisitor. "Do ye know what ye have risked in intruding here unbidden? What do ye know?"

"I know everything," replied the old man who first made his way in, speaking through the interpreter, and prostrating himself on the floor. "Let me speak! Let me speak for the love of God! There are a hundred more ready to say the same thing, and the Syud has sent me in time. Oh, my fathers, let us speak!"

"I protest against him," cried Dom Diego, with a hard, shrill voice, very different to his usual tone. "I denounce this as a conspiracy."

"We are the best judges of that," returned the Grand Inquisitor. "You, Diego di Fonseca, have already stated that you have no witnesses; and now, by a miracle as it were, one hath appeared suddenly, to whom credit may be given, a deacon of the Church. You can hear his statement and reply to it if you will. Let the Deacon Ramana be sworn and cautioned."

Meanwhile the old man was sworn, and his first act was to lay open the books he had brought and point to them as Maria's writing.

"Can you read these writings?" asked the Archbishop. "They are, I see, those which were confirmed by us after examination. I see my initials on every page."

"Surely, my Prince," replied the deacon. "When the priest is absent it is my duty to read such prayers and passages of Scripture as have been marked;" and, opening one of the books at random, he put on his large spectacles and began to read from the fifth chapter of the gospel according to Saint Matthew:—

"'Blessed are the poor in spirit, for theirs is the kingdom of heaven.'

"'Blessed are they that mourn, for they shall be comforted.'

"Shall I go on, my Prince? These words are so holy and comforting that few of the flock hear them without tears. I trust they are understood?"

"They are," replied the Grand Inquisitor; and, turning to Dom Diego, in a severe tone he continued, "and if this is the sorcery thou hast charged the prisoners with, thou hadst better be silent."

"And now," continued the old man, "I will speak for our blessed Padré, and tell what happened on the day that he took refuge at the Governor's. I have no fear of him," and he pointed to Dom Diego, "and have no charge to make against him; but the Lord and the blessed Virgin give me power to speak, and I am not afraid before them or you."

Then he related what he knew of the priest's plot. How he had engaged Beydurs and other lawless ruffians to carry off Maria; how on that Sunday night many of them had assembled at Moodgul, and one of them, being a friend of one of the shepherds, had told him what was to be done, and he went with some armed men to watch the Padré's church and house; how he heard Maria scream as she was alone singing vespers, and, looking in, saw her lying on the steps of the altar, and gave the alarm. We need not recapitulate all we already know; but the firmness and boldness of the narrator carried conviction with it to those who heard him. "And not only did I hear and see it all," he continued, "but these, my companions, know of it too, and will confirm it."

"God of heaven!" cried Dom Diego, casting up his hands, "I declare this to be a cónspiracy against me, instigated by the prisoners! Can it be believed in Thy holy sight? Surely Thou wilt blast their tongues ere they utter malignity against Thy servant!"

But the Court heeded him not; and the letters of Dom Diego were now laid out for all present to see them, and read, one by one, in a sonorous voice by the secretary; while the Archbishop and the secretary of the Holy Office brought forward large packets of documents from various parts of the Indies, of the handwriting of which there was no doubt, and which exactly corresponded with the Moodgul letters. That in relation to Doña Maria and her seduction caused a profound sensation through the assembly, and there were cries of "Let her explain! Let her explain!" from many.

"Let her swear what she likes," said the priest. "I only say these are forgeries made by herself to cover her own shame."

But this assertion, vague as it was, had no effect upon the tribunal. One by one the members compared all the letters with former documents. Many of them had maintained correspondence with the accused, and after an impressive silence, only broken by occasional whispers and communications among the members themselves—

"Do you know any of the associates of Dom Diego?" asked the Grand Inquisitor of the old deacon. "Speak truly and freely, but beware of slander or falsehood!" And this being interpreted to the old man, he broke forth at once.

"Know them? Yes; I know many. I know Pedro di Diaz, who used to come from Elias Khan, before Eyn-ool-Moolk, with money and letters, and I and many other people have seen him drinking with the Padré there. There was another man called Bartholomew, who sometimes came with him, and sometimes with others. All were rude, violent men. Diaz had the name of 'Pirate' among them. All of them kept out of our good Padré's way; and perhaps he never saw them—he was too innocent; but among ourselves we wondered at the profligacy that was carried on; not near the church, but in the bazaar of the town, where the great Padré used to come. One day one of the bankers in the city said to me, 'Your great Padré is very rich; I have exchanged fifty thousand rupees for him for bills on Panjim (Goa), and other bankers have also made remittances privately for him. 'Where does he get this money?' I said I could not tell, but it was reported everywhere that the Padré was a soldier in disguise, who was going to bring up Feringis and guns against Beejapoor. If that was to be kept secret, he had better not have trusted Pedro di Diaz, for he used openly to boast of it to many, and it became public talk. Does the Padré wish to ask me any questions? I will answer them, my princes, as truly as I have sworn to do upon the holy books and the holy water."

But Dom Diego made no reply. He had become ghastly pale, and his hands trembled.

"What did I or we care about all this?" continued the old man, excitedly; "but what we and every Christian man in our

Church did care for was the insult to our poor, kind, blessed, saint there, who ministered to our sick, taught our children, and helped her brother to write those blessed books. Ah, sirs! though we are but simple shepherds, yet our people have fought in many a frontier war; we have maintained our faith against Moslem and Hindoo, and in the cause of right fear no man. And I tell you, my princes, that had not Padré Francis enjoined peace upon us, we would have followed up Dom Diego that night, and brought him here to make him over to you."

"And why did Francis d'Almeida and his sister leave so suddenly?" he was asked.

"The citation to him had been read," replied the old man; "and after the service he told me he should have to go, and asked me to get him ponies to ride. In the evening, after the Señora's cruel insult, I took them temporarily to the palace of the Governor, Dilawar Khan, for I feared the Padré might return with the Beydurs and attack the Señora. Then, after a time, came an express from Beejapoor, and Dilawar Khan told them they must obey the Queen Chand's orders; and before daylight they were sent off to Juldroog in closed palanquins, whether they would or no. But for this they would have gone to you, for twenty-five well-armed youths of the congregation had volunteered their escort. Ah, sirs! it was a night of terror and alarm; and it was only when the Governor sent and put seals on everything, except these books, that we felt safe."

"We had not heard of this alleged insult before, daughter," said the Inquisitor; "and thou must speak to it, however painful, on pain of torture, to extort the truth, for this is a point which cannot be overlooked."

"My lords and illustrious fathers," said Maria, modestly, "if this truth had not transpired through the deacon I would have been silent, for I have innocence and my trust in the blessed Queen of Heaven to rely on; and whatever shame may appear in the narration belongs to him who caused it, not to me. We had never been intimate, as servants of the Church should be. My brother did not like what he heard, things he would not tell me of. I was pained by Dom Diego's licentious looks, and even, when in the Church, always sat near the children of my school. But one Sabbath evening he found me alone, teaching the children a hymn; and when they had gone he advanced towards me, and offered me such insult as no virtuous woman could endure, pressing his vile intentions with proposals to fly. And I sank down and fainted. I know not who rescued me, but when I was aroused I was at home again, and my brother, seizing his sword, rushed out to seek revenge, and was brought back; and I lay at the foot of my cross, praying that his hand should be withheld; and that was granted mercifully."

Bravely and calmly had Maria upheld her dignity and composure up to this period; but now she failed, and burst into hysterical sobs and tears, upheld by the abbess of her lay order, who had, with other sisters, accompanied her. But presently, and while all awaited her recovery, she rose, and holding out her pleading hands, cried—

"O fathers of the Church, as her child I come to you; as a woman who has been wounded in her honour I plead to you! There is not one spot of shame to my own perception upon my heart, and she can deliver me if I am true. If not, let the flame purge me, and may I be accepted! But leave me not to that vile man's machinations in after years."

She was not immediately replied to, and the tribunal took up the examination of Francis d'Almeida with new interest. He described their happy life at Moodgul, the affection and docility of the people, the progress he was making in Canarese with learned scholars of the place, his first essays in translation, and which he had sent for confirmation; and lastly, the insult to his sister. "If I could then and there have proceeded to you, holy fathers, I would have come; but a long journey needs several days' preparation, and I was without any notice considered a prisoner and sent to Beejapoor, where my innocence was proved to the satisfaction of its noble Queen by these letters of my coadjutor, which, she and her nephew, the King, have forwarded by their envoy. They are before ye, O fathers, and ye will judge whether the writing is mine or not."

Just then a messenger, who had been sent for Pedro di Diaz, returned and reported that his vessel had fallen down the river in the afternoon of the previous day, bound for Choule and Surat, and that Bartholomew Pinto, and others, with Diaz, were serving on board.

Then the Court was cleared for about an hour, for the day was fast declining; and, on the prisoners being again admitted, the Inquisitors rose as one man, while their chief cried with a loud voice, "Ye, Francis d'Almeida, and Maria de Pereira, we acquit and expurge ye from all accusation of heresy, sorcery, contempt, and other crimes with which ye have been charged; and ye go forth without shame or reproach to continue your labours as ye have done among the heathen.

"You, Dom Diego, member of the holy Society of Jesus, are found guilty, under your own handwriting, of falsehood and profligacy. You have insulted a virtuous and worthy daughter of the Church with infamous proposals. You have entered, as appears by your agreements, into an unholy and corrupt alliance with Moorish rebels to this kingdom; and you, by these papers, have acknowledged the receipt of vast sums of money. We condemn you, therefore, unless you make confession previously, to trial by the rack; and afterwards, on Sunday next, to death by fire, in order that the holy Church may be purged from your iniquity. Familiars, lead him forth; till the morrow he will have time to repent."

Dom Diego replied nothing. He well knew it was of no avail to appeal to those stony hearts which, whether just or unjust, never changed. He only bowed his head, muttered something that could not be distinguished, and was led into the great corridor whence the cells opened.

Can we describe the boundless thankfulness of the two who so lately were captives in the hands of that ruthless tribunal! As servants of God in their degrees, the brother and sister received the public blessings of the Archbishop and Grand Inquisitor; and, after that, falling into each other's arms, they wept like children before all. Before this, their feelings had been too highly strung to fail, but now they were weak with very excitement, and were considerately led back to their dwellings, to rest and receive those spiritual comforts in which their souls could now seek repose.

* * * * * *

"And thou wilt come at last, Balthasar," said Dom Diego, as having arrived at the end of the corridor, he turned into a door which was open, and revealed a small bed, with a loaf of bread and a jar of water. "Thou wilt not be long." Balthasar was Dom

Diego's cousin, who had been with him when he was formerly an officer of the Ajuba, and had taken charge of him.

"I will come," he said, "though I risk my life and brave the fire. I will come, and bring the rope for thee. If thou art strong and brave, as thou used to be, yon miserable window will have little terror for thee."

But Dom Diego had a surer plan in his mind than that.

"Oh, you need not bring a rope," he said; "I can manage without it, and it would betray you."

As his cousin entered shortly before midnight, and all the building was still, except for the wailings of wretches who sat alone in their misery, he closed the door, locking it inside. "Perhaps I can help you," he said, cheerfully.

"Yes," said Dom Diego. "No one can move those iron bars. You dare not leave the door open, but you can submit to be bound, and I will do it gently. Lie down there. Ha! thou wilt not," he said, from between his teeth. "Thou, too, a traitor!" And he then threw him down on the bed, and stuffed a large portion of his dress into his cousin's mouth. "Dare to stir, and I will kill thee. See, here is my old weapon!" and he drew a keen poignard from his breast. "Nay, that would be the surest way," and he seized the familiar by the throat.

"Mercy! Mercy! Diego!" gasped Balthasar. "Spare my life!

Oh, spare my life! Unshriven and unrepented, wouldst thou murder me?"

"Be still, then. If thou stir hand or foot, I will slay thee, Balthasar, as thou liest there; but be still, and I will not harm thee." Then Diego took off his cousin's robe, swathed the upper part of his person in the coarse sheet of the bed, and tearing his shirt into strips, with them and two handkerchiefs tied his legs together, so that they could not be moved. "There!" he cried, "that is the way we used to tie up the captives whom we carried off for ransom. Rest quietly there, my son, till some one finds thee in the morning; and thou must tell them they did not make so much of me as they might when I was here; they may find it hard to take me now. Addios, brother, I know my way out, and have a vow to attend midnight mass in the cathedral. How well thy robe fits me; perhaps thou wilt take mine in exchange. Addios! and pleasant dreams to thee this night, Balthasar. When thou wakest, tell Francis d'Almeida and his sister that I go to pursue them. Not till he is dead at my feet, and she grovels there in a shame worse than death, will I cease to dog them, hide where they may. Forget not!" and taking up the small lanthorn, he locked the door behind him, delivering a solemn benediction as he entered the corridor.

He knew his way perfectly. In years long before he had been one of the familiars, and knew every secret dungeon and torture chamber of the great building, every secret sign and password; and he made his way to the gate without opposition. The men on guard rallied him on going out so late; but he declared his vow of midnight mass, and passed on into the open air, unchallenged and unsuspected by his voice, for he had kept his cowl over his face, and his height corresponded so exactly with that of his cousin, that the detection of the imposture was impossible.

There was no one else in the square before the Ajua but a few stragglers, and Diego quietly found himself on the quay. One sailor was lying in the stern of the ship's boat, who was at once aroused, and slipped over the priest's shoulder a rough sailor's dress, and for a few moments was absent seeking his associates. One by one they emerged from their hiding place, gained the boat unobserved, and lay down in its bottom; and when the last one came he loosed the painter, took one of the oars, and sculled off leisurely towards the opposite shore. Near that, the men started up, took the oars, which were muffled, and rowed with all their power, and with a strong ebb tide made rapid way down to the sea, passing the forts without observation. The brigantine was not at anchor, but cruising to and fro, as if about to enter the river with the flood; but Dom Diego was soon on board, and before the fresh land wind the beautiful little vessel heeled over to the breeze and sped swiftly northwards.

## CHAPTER VIII.

### A DEATH, A MARRIAGE, AND A DEPARTURE.

WHEN morning broke there was much confusion in the great building. Balthasar, whose duty was to open the doors of the cells, was not to be found, nor were the keys hung up in their accustomed place. The door of Dom Diego's cell was, however, locked and bolted without as usual; but, on listening, a faint moaning sound was heard, and after some difficulty the massive door was opened, and Balthasar found as he had been left, though nearly suffocated. He had contrived to wriggle from the low pallet, but to free his hands and to release himself from his cousin's bandages had been impossible; nor could he loose the gag, for it had been tied securely behind, putting him to great pain and distress. Even to the suspicious Inquisitors there did not seem to be the least indication of complicity, and after a severe and prolonged examination, Balthasar was released. All that he could say was that he had been suddenly overpowered by his cousin, whose strength far exceeded his own; that he had been threatened with death, and even slightly wounded in the breast; that, on account of the gag, he could not cry out for aid. And even had he done so, who could have heard him among the wailings of other prisoners, and the cries and groans of those that were to endure the torture on the day following?

Then, under the information given by the old deacon, the transactions of the bankers of Panjim were examined by the civil and ecclesiastical authorities in conjunction. But no assets were found. They produced letters from Dom Diego remitting large sums by bills from Moodgul, and a considerable quantity of gold, and directing the whole, except a small portion to be kept for himself, to be paid to Pedro di Diaz, whom they knew as a trader to the East, and the owner of a remarkably fast-sailing brigantine, which he commanded. Some months before he had gone on a trading expedition with the Moors, and while some of the remittances belonged to him direct, others might have been the property of the Padré Sahib. It could only be conjecture, for it was no part of their business to inquire into their constituents' affairs; and for the rest, their books and vouchers were ample evidence. Finally, about four days before, the Captain Di Diaz had taken away all his money, partly in bills at sight, on Surat and Oman, but by far the greater part was in coin of various kinds, the majority being in gold. There was nothing to be made out of all this; nothing to afford the least clue to the course of the vessel Diaz commanded; or, indeed, that Dom Diego was with him, though it was supposed he might be; and he was never afterwards seen in Goa, nor did it ever transpire to the authorities there what had become of him. There was, however, long afterwards, a report prevalent that he had become a renegade from the Christian faith, and joined the ranks of the Mussulman army, and had fallen in some obscure battle.

It was a pleasant duty for the Archbishop to reward Francis d'Almeida for all the trials which had arisen out of his association with the bad man who had so narrowly escaped a horrible fate. But the more the prelate saw of the zealous missionary the more he appreciated his singular, and at that period nearly unknown, powers of translation, and the evident love and veneration in which he was held by his devoted flock. Could there be a greater proof of that than in the sturdy old deacon's journey from Moodgul to Goa unasked, on the mere supposition that the long threatened proceedings against his priest were to take place? This more, perhaps, than any other circumstance touched the prelate most deeply, and he was not slow to confess it.

In the cathedral a splendid high mass was solemnised for the delivery of Francis d'Almeida and his sister from the wicked machinations against them. Sermons were preached, setting forth their labours for many years, and the translations were exhibited on the altar steps to the public at large. The Viceroy bestowed a high order upon the priest at a banquet which was held in his honour; entertained the Beejapoor envoy very sumptuously;

and, from the simple communications of Francis d'Almeida, grew to have a higher respect for the kingdom than had ever been held by any Portuguese before.

Many arrangements about duties and trade generally were proposed; in fact, it appeared as though the present opportunity would throw open the two kingdoms to each other in a far more effectual and friendly manner. As to Doña Maria, we lose sight of her among her old friends, and the crowds of religious women who visited her. Many, indeed, volunteered to accompany her in her mission work, and teach in her schools; but European Portuguese, ignorant of any language but their own, could be of little use; and finally, before she left, she made choice of two of the sisters of her own convent, who, having been born in India, could speak the ordinary language of the western country with fluency.

Finally came the grand distinction, so unexpected, that Francis was completely overpowered by it. The Archbishop, having consulted privately with his council, considered it very advisable to extend the mission, and to consolidate its several points under one head. At present there were but four churches, two under Moodgul, and two under Raichore; but there was a good chance of the establishment of one at Beejapoor, and perhaps another at Ahmednugger, under the auspices of Queen Chand Beebee. It was advisable, therefore, that Francis d'Almeida should be created bishop, with permission to travel and preach wherever he thought most advisable.

At first, as we have said, the worthy priest was overwhelmed, and requested time for consideration ; but it appeared both to him and to Maria, and to their best friends, that the honour and the responsibility could not be evaded. And again, if he declined it, neither of them would be sent to carry out the Archbishop's plans. Now, there was no one who knew the people or their language, manners, and customs, at all so well ; no one who could compete with the Mussulmans and Brahmins on their own grounds of theology. He was, too, used to the courtly manners and modes of life of the Mussulman who ruled the country, and was the intimate friend of Queen Chand and her nephew, the King. What would not Taj-ool-Nissa do for the physician who had aided her recovery, or for the beloved companion who had cheered her loneliness ? Then, again, there were Meeah and Zóra, the old Syud, and their new schools at the painter's, and great numbers of other countrymen who had been absent with the King's army, and were altogether fallen into neglect. All these were new ties which a series of strange events had created, but which, nevertheless, were precious and binding. And these, with the boundless expanse of country before him, in which he should be free to act, caused Francis d'Almeida's heart to swell in grateful anticipation. He, therefore, submitted himself to the Archbishop's will, with earnest and sincere feelings of gratitude; and as soon as the ceremony could be arranged, he was consecrated in the cathedral at high mass, before all the ecclesiastical, civil, and military authorities of the city, and his patent made out and delivered to him. Nor would the Archbishop suffer him, poor as he knew Francis was, to pay any of the costs of the elevation, which were considerable; not even that of his robes, which were of their kind splendid enough.

The Beejapoor envoy was a delighted spectator of all the pomp of the Church on the occasion, and the joy with which he greeted his former humble companion was very genuine. We are bound to say also, that once they were free from the terrors of the Inquisition, Maria, like a practical woman as she was, insisted upon making a complete inspection of her brother's wardrobe, and found it in a very dilapidated and defective condition. The patchings and darnings of old Pedro, who nominally united the office of tailor to that of cook and valet, were by no means of a distinguished order, and were, to say the least of them, in the last stage of decay; and in the cold weather of the Dekhan, her brother, though enjoying wonderfully good health, was often distressed by the cold. Materials, however, and makers of all kinds were plentiful at Goa. The ladies of her convent set to with vigour to make such portions of both their clothing as they could, and the result was so far beyond the good Padré's ordinary ideas of comfort, which were limited, that he could barely be induced to cast away the old and to adopt the rich new suits with which he was furnished.

They were pressed much to remain for the great Church festival of Christmas. But this was impossible; time was precious; the Beejapoor envoy and his people were anxious to return, and the journey back was commenced. What peril they had endured and escaped, what new honour and love they had gained, was indeed wonderful to think on, and for which their thanks were due to Him whom they served; and their hearts were full of gratitude and hope for the future. And the reception they had at Beejapoor, when Humeed Khan and his nephew, with a host of other friends, one of the King's nobles of the court, ushers and others, were sent out to meet them and conduct them into the city, was almost overwhelming; and many people ran before their litters, crying out that the good Padré had come back, and was welcome. As to the children of the schools, they and their parents erected a triumphal arch of a humble character at Pedro the painter's gate; and, dressed in their best, sang a hymn of welcome very prettily, and were introduced to their new preceptresses. Pedro had made a great feast for the occasion too, and all were very happy; but they were grieved to hear that their dear old friend the Syud was rapidly sinking to his rest, and that the physicians had no longer hope of his life. Prayers had been made for him in every mosque, and supplications sent to all other shrines around, particularly to Gulburgah. But these were of no avail; the angel of death, the old man said, was already nigh, and he should soon receive his last summons. Weary nature was exhausted; and though the few last months' excitement had caused the lamp of life to flicker up, and even to shine brightly for awhile, it was now sinking daily, and must soon be extinguished.

They did not delay further than to make a few arrangements. The King and the Queen had already sent kind messages, begging them to come as soon as possible; and in the afternoon they went when the usual palanquins arrived for them. They found Abbas Khan, his uncle, and a number of Mussulman priests, sitting in the ante-room of the old Syud's apartments, the latter chanting passages from the Koran in a low monotonous tone; and while Maria passed into Zóra's rooms, Abbas Khan rose, and led the bishop, as we must now call him, into the place where the dear old man lay. He seemed to be dozing as they entered, but hearing the sound of a strange voice, he looked up and asked who had come.

"I, your old friend, Huzrut," said the bishop, kneeling down. "I have returned to you safe from my journey and its consequences."

"Oh, give me light that I may see you once more ere I pass

away," he said, eagerly. "Give me light!" and when a corner of the curtain was lifted, the old man raised himself, stretched out his hands, and fell upon his friend's neck. He seemed to have forgotten that he was blind.

"The darkness and the day are all one to me, my son," he said, feeling all over Francis' face; "all one now—so they are always to those who are trembling on the brink of eternity. Yet I shall see brightly presently, when these scales of death fall from my eyes. Fear not for me, dear friend; my time is run, my work on earth is finished, and I go to partake of that I have believed in. And thou hast escaped that fierce evil priest? Tell me how it was. First lay me down, for I have no strength."

"You must not speak," was the reply; "it excites you too much;" and D'Almeida placed his fingers on the old man's pulse, which he found now weak and fluttering. "Rest awhile, and I will tell thee."

"Is he dying?" asked Abbas Khan.

"No," returned the bishop; "he will yet live some days; and I will send him or bring him early some cordial I have brought with me. Now no one can get at it."

"Now tell me all, Francis; and how thy dear sister, Maria, hath fared. Is she well?"

"She is well," returned the bishop; "but I have said you must be silent;" and he then related briefly the particulars of the investigation of the tribunal. "I could have done nothing," he said; "he was more powerful than I; but I had truth with me, and out of his own vile letters he was condemned; nor could he make any defence. He was sentenced, and would have suffered, but he escaped."

"Escaped! Protection of God! he may follow you and Maria."

"I do not fear him, Huzrut. The same power that defended us at Goa will defend us should we meet hereafter. Meanwhile, he fled in a companion's ship to sea, and is believed to have gone to Persia, where we have churches. He escaped, too, with all his wealth."

"Shookr! shookr! thanks, thanks! and praise to God that our poor prayers were heard; prayers in which Zóra joined, as for brother and sister. Hast thou no thanks, no congratulations, Meeah?"

"I said them at first, Abba, when he told me on the road. But see the justice of God! On all that number of vile conspirators justice hath descended. And on this priest last of all, though he hath life and wealth, yet shame hath fallen upon him among his people; while this, our honoured friend, hath been exalted by them to high rank, and is now a noble of the Church."

"He is no greater now before me than he used to be, nor before God. Is he, too, a Wallee?"

"Not a saint, Abba," returned Francis, smiling; "but I have the overlooking of all the churches from Ahmednugger to Raichore and Moodgul, and can reside where I please. Before God I cannot change, but before men I have that dignity in the Church which it hath pleased my fathers in God to bestow upon me."

The old man smiled happily, and they saw his lips moving silently in prayer; but he did not speak, he only held out his hands once to Francis, as if to bid him farewell, and turning round seemed to sleep easily and comfortably.

Zóra and Maria were together once more, and what could exceed their happiness? Zóra's great brown eyes looked wistfully at her, like a dog's, as after the first weeping and thankful embrace they sat down together. But this did not suffice, and as Maria held out her arms once more, Zóra fell into them, looking up every now and then with her happy, loving face, though her eyes were constantly brimming over, as she heard Maria's history, as Abba had heard her brother's. Only about three months had passed, yet Zóra's figure and countenance appeared to have expanded under the influence of the certainty of Meeah's love. At last her own, her very own. "And he loves me, too; for one day I was coming from the Queen Mother's apartment alone, and I met him on the stairs, and he told me so; and though I could not answer him, I remember all he said, and now I can tell it to you, Maria. We have never spoken again; and I dare not if I could, for it would not be modest in a girl betrothed to do so. Then Abba began to fail after you left, and yearned for your brother; and we thought he would pass away from us. But he is still here, though they tell me he may be called any time; and we must let him go. Day and night Meeah watches him, and when he is tired he sends me word by a servant, and I go to him. But he seldom speaks, only prays; and all he has been saying for several days has been: 'It is time they returned. Why do they linger away? Have they escaped?' But we could not make out then, though we now understand your peril." And then Zóra's tongue ran on almost without intermission, until a message came from the Queen Mother that they should go up to them, as she and the young Queen were both ready to receive them. And they went; Maria kissing the feet of both the Royal ladies, and making her obeisance, as she used to do. They, too, had to hear of her trial and her deliverance; and Zóra said plaintively, "We were sisters together from the first, though we belonged to different faiths; and God appointed me my trial, when I did not fear Osman Beg, and she had her own with the wicked priest we used all to hear so much of in Juldroog; and she was not afraid of him. And now God hath brought us together again; and we will never separate."

Then the Queen had to hear of Francis d'Almeida's new dignity; and it was very clear to Maria that he, perhaps both of them, had acquired additional honour in the Royal eyes.

"My King will be glad, indeed, to hear this, for Beejapoor hath never had an ambassador from your nation, or any accredited person on whom reliance could be placed; and much mischief has been the consequence. Now things will be different."

"I know," said Maria, smiling, "that he has been entrusted with a whole budget of matters to lay before His Majesty; and he will do this to-night, perhaps, at the durbar."

"And," added Zóra, with a merry twinkle in her eye, "bid him, mother, to come in his new robes, for Maria says they are magnificent; and then he can come and make his obeisance here also to you and his old patient."

So, after a while, Maria took her leave, and went home to carry out this little plot, and to set out her brother's finery; and, after much persuasion, the simple bishop did as he had been requested, and went in his grandeur of gold embroidery and purple satin, and lace, and biretta instead of a mitre, which, with his staff, was not ready when he left Goa. He was, however, sufficiently splendid to attract the attention and admiration of all the nobles of the durbar; and even the Chishtee priest, who had been so uncivil to him at their first meeting, but who had gradually learned to respect his character, now welcomed him with sincere congratulations.

It was a pleasant evening for the Bishop. He felt himself to be now more on an equality with all the nobles by whom he was surrounded, and their respect was unmistakeable. He was the representative of his nation, too; there was much to be settled between his Government and the King's; and in all respects, in outward circumstances, he felt he was a very different person at the King's Court than the obscure priest and physician that had come there at first. The schools were flourishing, and Maria felt the help of her new assistants to be very material. The Bishop, too, found ample occupation among the Portuguese artificers and gunners, and the time was fast approaching when he must seek his new flocks at Ahmednugger and elsewhere. Would it be safe or prudent to take his sister with him? What he heard of the condition of Ahmednugger was not satisfactory. The place was not at peace within itself, and many reports were abroad. He had a refuge for her already at Beejapoor, or he might send her to Moodgul, to the old deacon's charge; but the last message of Dom Diego to his cousin, which had been duly repeated to him as a warning, though Maria knew not of it, often weighed heavily upon him. Dom Diego was free; free to join any lawless bands in the country; and he had wealth, too, to further any plan he might form. In Beejapoor Maria would be safe, under the King's protection; but then the dire separation, distressing alike to both, was hardly to be contemplated. Maria would not hear of it; whither he would go she would go with him, and in her opinion the better plan was to wait till Ahmednugger was once more settled.

But all these plans were destined to come to a more rapid end than either thought; and the first link of the chain broken, was the dear old Syud's death. For several days the new medicine which Francis had brought with him appeared to give new energy, and they all hoped he might rally; but he was not himself deceived. "I have received my warning," he said, "and do but wait the angel's coming—be that when it may." He made his will, bequeathing to Zóra all his worldly goods and such of his estates as the King might permit. He also made provision for the religious ceremonies at his tomb, the site of which he had selected when he first came, in the Roza, or garden, in the precincts of the great mausoleum of the King, and had appointed a poor disciple, who had followed him in his wanderings from Gogi, to the charge of it. A small tomb or mausoleum, with a vault, had been prepared, and was nearly finished; and the old man on one of his best latter days had been gently taken there in a palanquin, having a particular desire to see it. To the last he preserved his faculties entire; and after hearing portions of the Koran read one night, he repeated the two creeds with a firm voice, and lay down quietly. But his breath came heavily, and Abbas Khan saw that the end was near; and Zóra came to him with Maria, who was sitting with her. The physicians and Francis felt his pulse, but it was fluttering; and one of the Moollas raising him up, poured a little sherbet into his mouth, which he swallowed and lay down again, saying, "It is enough," and seemed to sleep; nor could those who watched by him tell when the humble, loving spirit left its earthly tenement. There was no struggle, or even a sigh; and again and again during the day he had said he had no pain, and could see the flowers of Paradise and the river flowing among them. Finally the chant of the Moollas without ceased, and those who perform offices for the dead came in and did their ministering. Crowds followed him to his last resting place. Nothing that love or respect could suggest was wanting to the end; and as the Moollas chanted the peace of God to the thousands who had gathered round, they separated sadly, many weeping, and with a conviction that a faithful disciple of their faith had gone to his rest in Paradise.

For a time, during the forty days of ceremonial and mourning, Zóra remained with the Queen Dowager, though apart, so as not to cause inconvenience; and for the first few days Maria had not left her except at short periods, and to carry on her own duties. She had now many friends; and the grief at her loss, which at first lay heavy on her, gradually gave place to brighter thoughts. Often and humbly did she think on the few months that had passed, on the hopelessness which must have been her lot if her grandfather had died at Juldroog or during her wanderings. Yes, she had been mercifully protected, and was grateful to her heart's core; and as she wept out her grief on Maria's breast or that of the Queen, who had adopted her, there was ever present the secret hope and trust that she had found a true refuge, which was not far distant. For as the forty days of ceremonial were about to conclude, the Lady Fatima, urged by her nephew and husband, again protested against further delay. Zóra should have one who had a right to protect her, and in whose love a new life would open to her, and she put herself unreservedly into her friends' hands. She had pledged her faith, and had she needed to do so a hundred times over, or under any trial, she would have only been more confirmed in it. Enough that the time was come; and with all the pomp that her Royal patrons and the wealthy house of her husband could furnish, all the dressing, feasting, merry-making, processions, and distributions of charity practised on such occasions, the marriage ceremonies were at last concluded. Are not the loves of this happy pair sung by bards and dancing-women to this day? For the poets of the Court poured forth their amatory lays and epithalamiums without stint, sure of ample largesse. Many of these were set to music, and linger still to charm others, though even the traditions of the nobles of Beejapoor have passed away.

And still the good Bishop and Maria remained. Maria pleaded that she had promised Zóra to stay with her till the ceremonies were completed, and she, with much interest, and not without amusement, had helped her through all the events of each day.

But when all was over, when the bright, radiant, happy girl had been carried away in a grand procession, with fireworks, torches, and firing of guns, escorted by the whole of her husband's and his uncle's household troops—the play played out, and the curtain dropped—then they turned to their work again.

Meanwhile the Queen's letters from Ahmednugger grew more and more uneasy; and she received a petition, which was signed by all the principal nobles and officers of the State, asking her to come to them and assume the administration during the minority of the young and rightful Sovereign, who as yet was little more than an infant. This was necessarily a much more serious subject for contemplation than the heretofore task of assuaging national disquietude, and uniting the power of the State under one regency, not her own, which should have the goodwill of the people. But this was put before her as a solemn and patriotic duty, which could be effected by no one but herself. At her name, they wrote in her native city, every well affected person would unite to support her; the few malcontents would disappear or fly the kingdom, and peace and prosperity would reign once more. Day by day, by special messengers, and by every other possible means, the frequency of these communications, as well as their urgency, increased. They had commenced before Francis and his sister had returned from Goa, and were much more frequent and more urgent now.

She had concealed nothing from her nephew, the King, or from his long tried and faithful Ministers of State. Every letter, every despatch she received, was laid before them; but the last general petition seemed to leave no loophole of escape. So long as Ahmednugger was disturbed, Beejapoor could not be at rest. The frontiers were uneasy, and events took place which no precaution could avert, and which might at any time plunge the kingdoms into one of those interminable and bloody wars which had often nearly brought both to the brink of ruin. The last war was finished, peace everywhere prevailed, and under ordinary circumstances, there was every prospect of its maintenance; but if misrule at Ahmednugger continued, there was no surety. Again, the Moghuls of Delhi were gathering in ominous clouds in Malwa and Guzerat, without apparent reason; and were they to march upon the Dekhan, there was no one to resist them on its frontiers; while at Ahmednugger each party seemed ready to sell their country to the enemy, so that a temporary local advantage might be gained.

It was a perilous time for the whole Dekhan; and the Queen, with her habitual fortitude, determined to meet it, as she had done every political and public danger of her life. She would devote herself to her native State, for her presence was no longer needful at Beejapoor, and her Regency had closed in thankful peace. Nay, there was no time to be lost, and it was at once known, by the preparations ordered, that Queen Chand was about to proceed to her native place. We need not say that Abbas Khan and Zóra were to accompany her. They would take no denial, and Abbas Khan, in public durbar, claimed the command of her escort, as a point of right and duty. Could he leave his adopted mother, and idle away his time in inaction at the capital? Even that he had endured since the King's return had been in the last degree irksome. We know why the Bishop and his sister desired to go too; and even had that reason not existed, Maria must have gone, for the Queen had become alarmed, and she viewed with pain a revelation the King had made to her that he loved Maria.

As the time drew near for her departure, the Queen Chand had received many visits from her nephew the King, and had observed his listless manner and his evident anxiety in regard to some subject. He did not, however, complain of being ill, and his Queen, Taj-ool-Nissa, had, as well as the Queen Dowager, pressed him to consult the good Bishop on the subject. To both the Queens, the departure of the elder one, on whose counsel in all affairs he had so firmly relied, appeared to be the cause; but it lay deeper than that.

One evening, just before the march began, the Queen, Taj-ool-Nissa and Maria were sitting at the great window alone, and Maria was putting the last finishing touches to a drawing of flowers for her Royal companion, when she observed the te.rs well up in her eyes; and, with a sudden impulse, she put the drawing aside, and cast herself upon Maria's breast, sobbing piteously. It was in vain that Maria asked her to explain the cause of her grief, or tried to soothe her with assurances of speedy return, the Queen only wept the more passionately.

"He does not love me, Maria," she said, between her sobs, in broken words. "My lord the King does not love me. To thee, O sister, he has given his heart, and he will die without thee. I am but a child, Maria, and have no beauty or talent to charm him; but thy loveliness and accomplishments fit thee to become his Queen. Oh, do not hesitate, darling sister; consent to be mine in reality, and we shall be joined in his love till we die. Maria!" she cried, looking up through her tears, and brushing them away, "dost thou hear? He dreams of thee; I hear thy name on his lips as he sleeps, murmured in love. It is no deception, and I say it before God; and I know how essential thou art to his happiness. Kiss me, and say thou wilt consent, and I shall be happy. A few quiet prayers and some preparation, and thou art his wife as well as I."

"It cannot be, it cannot be, my darling!" said Maria, very sadly, and kissing the gentle, patient face upturned to her. "I am vowed to God's service; I repeated and confirmed those vows at Goa, and I go forth, with my brother, to perform them. A little while and he will forget me, and thou wilt live with thy child to come, happy in his love as thou hast been. Nay, urge me not," she continued, as Taj-ool-Nissa was about to speak again; "by the love that is between us urge me not again, but let me depart in peace, and with thy blessing, on my way. Keep this, and all I have left, in memory of me; and hope, as I do, that we may meet again in happiness." Then, placing the picture in the Queen's hands, she kissed her fervently, with a silent prayer, and, rising up, departed. Yet ere she reached the door, she looked back once more. The girl was lying with her face among her cushions, weeping bitterly, while the sun's light, falling upon her rich brocaded dress, covered her as with a glory of gold.

END OF BOOK IV.

# BOOK V.

## CHAPTER I.

### A SKETCH OF LOCAL HISTORY.

OUT of the disruption of the great Bahmuny dynasty of the Dekhan in A.D. 1489, four independent kingdoms arose. The first secession was that of Yousaf Adil Khan, who founded the Adil Shahy dynasty of Beejapoor in that year; the second, that of Nizam-ool-Moolk Bheiry, in the same year, and Berar had even preceded them. Golconda followed in 1512, thus completing the alienation of the four largest and most important provinces of the Bahmuny kingdom, and leaving only a comparatively insignificant portion in the hands of the remaining representative of the Bahmunies, who lived and reigned at Beeder, and whose successor was afterwards set aside by his Minister, Ameer Bereed, who usurped the throne, and the great Bahmuny family became extinct.

Nizam-ool-Moolk Bheiry had been Prime Minister of the Bahmuny kingdom, and his son, Mullek Ahmud, was Viceroy in the large western provinces. After the act of dismemberment had been accomplished, Nizam-ool-Moolk Bheiry died, and his son, relying on his local power, and possessing the requisite boldness and ability, ably maintained his position; and there being no capital to the province except the hill fort of Joonair, which was inconvenient, as well from position as construction, he founded a new city and capital near the village of Bingar, which lay between Joonair and Dowlutabad.

Here he built a fine fort and several palaces, laid out gardens, and named the place Ahmednugger—or the fort of Ahmud—which appellation it still bears. Ahmednugger is now one of the large military stations of the Dekhan and of India, and is deservedly celebrated for its salubrious climate. It is, in fact, situated near the crest of one of the great trap waves of the Dekhan, which breaks into the valley of the Godavery, a few miles distant. The country around is open, fertile, and free from jungle; and in the times we write of, the position commanded the passes from Khandeish, and Guzerat, and Berar, into central Dekhan. It had been most judiciously chosen; and, while the kingdom endured, it ruled a fair country which stretched from the sea to the confines of Berar and Golconda, and was possessed of an ample revenue. Its people, too, were the sturdy Mahratta peasantry, who made excellent soldiers; and it maintained considerable bodies of Abyssinians, as well as Turks, Arabs, Persians, and Central Asians, and their descendants of mixed blood, who, as at Beejapoor, were called

Dekhanies, and held much power in their hands. In this point therefore the two kingdoms were very similar, though local customs and parties might not be in all respects precisely so. The Ahmednugger State also employed the indigenous Mahratta soldiery to a much greater extent than Beejapoor, especially as cavalry, and frequently found them of great use in checking the turbulence of the foreign levies. They were considered a portion of the regular army, and thus the hereditary native chieftains of the Mahratta people rose to power, which was afterwards rendered conspicuous when the Mahratta people, living upon the ruins of the local Mussulman kingdoms, became a nation in themselves.

We do not purpose to write the history of the Nizam Shahy kingdom. The Kings were rough, warlike, and quarrelsome with their neighbours beyond any others, and were very rarely at entire peace with any of them. And while in some of these wars the kingdom had narrowly escaped annihilation, yet because a balance of power among these kingdoms was necessary for mutual existence, no one of them could be annexed by another, and for more than a hundred years they had existed in pretty much the same condition as that in which they had commenced in 1489.

They had of course intermarried, and the families for the most part were nearly related; but the principal event of this kind was the marriage of Chand Beebee, daughter of Hussein Nizam Shah, of Ahmednugger, in 1564, to Ally Adil Shah, of Beejapoor, in order to cement the political alliance between the States, on the occasion of the crusade against the Hindoo powers of northern India. And though the object of that coalition and campaign was fully carried out, yet the peace of the two kingdoms was by no means assured; and we have already had to trace the cause of wars which ended in the death in action of King Ibrahim Nizam Shah, the seventh King, in the field of battle near Puraindah. After this event the affairs of the unfortunate kingdom fell gradually into greater and greater confusion. There was no successor of mature age to succeed; and a boy, said to have been of Royal birth, was sent for from Dowlutabad and placed on the throne under the auspices of the Dekhany party and their chieftain. But this was opposed by the foreign faction, who claimed that the infant son of the late King should succeed. As usual, both parties betook themselves to arms, and many lamentable and bloody engagements took place, not only in and near the Royal city itself, but also in other parts of the Ahmednugger dominions; the result of which was the general appeal to the Dowager Queen, Chand Beebee, to come to Ahmednugger, assume the Regency, and govern the kingdom with her well-tried ability and sagacity on behalf of the minor Prince; and, as we know, she had, after many deep considerations, consented to do so.

There was, however, a more pressing, and, to the Queen's perception, more dangerous crisis at hand. The Emperor Akhbar, of Dehli, who was gradually annexing all smaller independent dominions to his own empire, had already shown a desire for interference in Dekhan affairs. He had despatched a large army under his son the Prince Moorad to Guzerat and Malwa, to watch the course of Dekhan events, and to invade the country should he find pretext or opportunity for doing so; and of this invasion the Queen was in dread. Domestic broils and disagreements had before on many occasions been adjusted, but the presence of so powerful a force as the Great Moghul's army, in the distracted state of local politics, was an evil which could not be overrated. Already the leader of the Dekhany party was known to have addressed letters to the Prince Moorad, imploring his intervention to uphold the claims of the boy whom he had placed on the throne; and it was impossible to conceive that the astute Prince would neglect the very opportunity he had so long waited for. True, afterwards the Dekhany leader perceived and bitterly regretted the false step he had taken, more especially when the boy whom he supported had been discovered to be spurious. But the mischief done was irreparable, and the Queen Regent now knew that she should not only have to subdue local disaffection, but oppose the progress of the Imperial Prince with all the force and all the energy she could command.

She had undertaken the duty, however, and cast ease and other personal considerations unselfishly aside. She had done what she could for Beejapoor, and was wanted there no longer, except to make part of her nephew's happiness and share in his prosperity. And now, if in days of advancing age she was again to be thrown into those scenes of war which had accompanied her early life, it was, she said, the will of God and her duty; and she bowed to both with a submission and fortitude which never deserted her to the last.

We trust the foregoing sketch of the period, as far as Ahmednugger is concerned, will not be out of place. Without it, indeed, the course of this tale would hardly be intelligible.

## CHAPTER II.

### A PLEASANT JOURNEY.

THE first halt made by the Queen was at Sholapoor, which, formerly belonging to Ahmednugger, had been given to Beejapoor as part of her dowry on the occasion of her marriage; and the Royal lady once more took possession of the small but elegant suite of apartments which look out on the lake or tank which washes the eastern side of the fort, and was evidently intended as part of its defences. Sholapoor, for the most part, has even now no pretensions to beauty, and the country around it, and that which had been traversed since the Queen left Beejapoor, is bare and monotonous; but the immediate vicinity of the fort, including the lake, with its island covered by a large Banian tree and a Hindoo temple, is undoubtedly pretty; and the pleasant sound of the tiny wavelets as they plashed against the walls and bastions was refreshing to hear, while the wind which played over the water came through the windows which looked over the lake very refreshingly. The Queen did not, however, tarry here, nor did she take the direct road from Sholapoor by the valley of the Seena to Ahmednugger. It was not only hot, but the country had been wasted by the previous war, and had not had time to recover; she, therefore, turned eastward to Nuldroog, or Shahdroog, as it had been called by her husband, Ali Adil Shah, and which he had improved by new fortifications and a noble dam of masonry across the river, a place in which many of the happiest hours of her life had been spent while the great works were in progress.

Nuldroog, for it has reverted to its own old name, occupies a crest or knoll of basalt, which juts from the main plateau into the deep valley of the small river Boree. After passing the narrow neck which connects it with the plateau, the knoll spreads out with a tolerably level surface, the north, east, and south sides being for the most part perpendicular; while the neck, through which a wide and deep ditch has been cut, is fortified by a heavy wall with curtains and bastions. These walls and bastions continue all round the crest of the precipice, and the result has been a very strong fort of an eminently picturesque character, which might not make much defence against modern artillery, but which at the time we write of was considered one of the strongholds of the country, and usually held a large garrison, especially of cavalry. And it was an important military position, too, serving to check the forces of Ahmednugger on the one hand and Golconda on the other.

King Ali Adil Shah had done much for the place. Besides the

strengthening of the fortifications, and building near the east end a huge cavalier upwards of ninety feet high, ascended by a broad flight of easy steps, he had built a dam of stone and mortar of great strength and beauty across the river, which held back the waters, and created a long, narrow, but deep lake, which gave a plentiful supply of water to the town and both ends of the fort. Before this the only water procurable had been from the bed of the river, which flowed in the bottom of the deep ravine below the fort, and which in the hot weather was very scanty and impure. The new dam, therefore, gave a new value to the strong fort, and water became not only plentiful but easy of access. It is a noble work, stretching from one rocky point of the valley to another beyond, upwards of a hundred yards in length, and upwards of ninety feet in height. Over this the river falls in an unbroken sheet when in flood ; at other times, the surplus water is carried off by a channel formed in the crest of the dam, which falls into the large deep pool that has been hollowed out at the foot. By an ingenious contrivance, a pretty Gothic apartment has been left in the body of the work, over the windows of which the waters in the highest floods can pass without entering, as they are diverted from the top down a tunnel, and escape at the base. At the northern end of the dam is another fort, or *tête-du-pont*, formed by the fortification of a considerable knoll, which is in itself a strong position, and materially assists the other defences.

It was a great delight to the Queen to revisit the place. The Governor's house was cleared out for her, and for several days the whole fort was made private; and she wandered from place to place with her companions and attendants every day, pointing out to Maria and Zóra where she had sat for hours together with her lord the King, watching the works in progress, breathing the pure fresh air, and taking their simple meals on the top of a bastion, or on the high cavalier when it was finished, where a great canopy used to be pitched. Nor was it possible for the two girls not to be interested in the place itself. It was, indeed, very beautiful: the lake shimmering in the sun, with the black precipices, hung with many-hued creepers, reflected into it; while, after it had shot through the arch on the dam, the river brawled down the valley till it was hid from view by the projection of the hills below. The air here was cool and refreshing, for they had risen to a considerable height above Sholapoor: and this was another reason why the Queen had chosen the upper route instead of the lower. Here and there, from points on the table land without the fort, where the Queen took her companions, the dim blue plains of Beejapoor could be seen stretching to the horizon like a sea, and the fresh cool wind would come to them freely and soothingly. These, too, were old haunts of her husband and herself; and it seemed often to Maria and Zóra that, in the dreamy mood of mind in which she often sat alone, she appeared like one who had a consciousness of seeing these well-remembered scenes for the last time, and carrying away every possible recollection of them in her loving heart. Often, indeed, she would draw one or other, or both of them, to her side, and with her eyes brimming with tears, would say, "Look, children! here my lord received such a letter, or told me such a thing, and you must not forget even a stone of it; but, should I ask you even when my eyes are dim in death, you must describe it all to me as you see it now in the bright glowing sunlight."

I need not follow minutely the daily march in early cool morning, nor the succession of beautiful mango groves in which the party rested every day, affording cool shade and refreshing rest. They were, indeed, seldom in their tents till nightfall, for around the enclosure was a screen of tent walls, which made the whole private. The tent pitchers selected the shadiest portions of these groves, and usually contrived to enclose a number of large leafy trees, beneath which carpets and soft cushions were spread; and reading, or the Queen's business, with her clever secretary, Zóra, who had gained confidence by experience, went on as usual; and embroidery, too, and Maria's paintings, except when she retired to her own tents to share her devotions with her brother; while overhead the birds chirped, or sang, or cooed, and screamed in their glee and freedom.

To Zóra in her new happiness this march was a perpetual

elysium. Abbas Khan could not always be with her, for he had his own work to do in the regulation of the camp, the obtaining of supplies, and the payment for them, and all other current business. Sometimes, too, and indeed generally of an evening, the large Royal tent was opened; and the Queen received in durbar all the officers, zemindars, and chief inhabitants of villages around. The Queen had quitted the dominions of Beejapoor soon after leaving Nuldroog, and passed into those of Ahmednugger. Abbas Khan by no means liked what he heard from all quarters in regard to the position of Ahmednugger and the parties there, who seemed to be at constant and bloody feud; and he earnestly strove with the Queen to induce her to turn back. But she upbraided him. "Would she have the world think her a coward? and had she not brought Beejapoor through worse troubles than those?" So he was silent thenceforth. It was her fate, and whatever was to be, would be fulfilled.

The leader of the Dekhany party, Mean Munjoo, who had set up the spurious prince, was not at Ahmednugger. He had taken the boy with him, and gone beyond Owsa, towards Golconda, to urge the necessity of supporting Ahmednugger; and he was bitterly repentant that he had invited the Prince Moorad. He wrote to the Queen for forgiveness, and declared he would not return except with troops from Golconda and Beejapoor, to drive the Moghuls back. The Queen, too, wrote to her nephew, King

Ibrahim, to send a heavy force of cavalry, in which the Moghuls were said to be weak, and to watch affairs from Nuldroog; and subsequently as many as twenty-six thousand of the best cavalry of Beejapoor, with six thousand from Golconda, assembled there, and occupied the crests of the plateau which stretched northwards.

With these precautions taken, which had occasioned several days' delay at Patoda, the Queen now marched on, faster than before, for it was impossible to overrate the importance of her presence at Ahmednugger. But it was the same pleasant journey throughout, the same succession of cool, shady groves and crisp bracing air. Often would the Queen wile away the march with her hunting leopards and falcons with her, and enjoy many a gallop over the undulating downs, where Abbas Khan and the officers of his small force, and even the good Bishop, would ride with her and enjoy the sport. Sometimes, too, Maria, when the march was a quiet one, rode with her brother, to the great envy of Zóra, who, from an elephant allotted to her, looked after them as they cantered past her, longing to be with them. If there were anything remarkable to be seen, the Queen would diverge from the beaten track, as she did at the temple of Pukrode, and, looking over the crest, could follow the line of hills to Ahmednugger itself. There she had stayed an extra day to wander about, as was her wont, and enjoy the keen air of that elevation, which, while it put roses into Maria's cheeks, and made Zóra ruddy, tinged even the Queen's pale countenance with pink, and restored the bright beauty of her youth. Again from Patoda they made a day's excursion to the waterfall of the Incherna and its gloomy abrupt ravine; and they would sit for hours on the short smooth sward above, and watch the rainbows playing over the pool, nearly four hundred feet below them, and those which seemed to start out suddenly from the column of water, flash for an instant, and disappear. How glorious it all was! Even the heavy state cares which weighed upon the Queen seemed to be put aside for the time; and the noble lady's cheerful, nay, even playful disposition diffused a joy among her little party which they had never felt before. To Zóra it was perfect elysium, as she told her husband in their quiet hours; she often felt her heart too full for speech. "I had hoped, dear lord, to be happy with thee, and to make thee happy; but this reality transcends all my expectations, for you are all too kind and too indulgent to me."

"No, Zóra; all the love which inspired me as thou watched over me that first night doth but heighten by time. When I had it not, I hungered and thirsted for it. Now I have it, it groweth fresher every day, and more precious to me. Enjoy these happy days, therefore, to the full, for the time cometh, I fear me, in which there may be weeping and woe."

"Why dost thou think so?" she asked.

"I read much in the mother's sweet face," he returned. "When she gazes on these scenes of her old happiness, there is a wistful, lingering look in her eyes which seems to say, 'I am looking at ye for the last time.' When she rises to depart, it is not with a merry remark, as it used to be, but with a sigh and a silent tear, which I can read, though you may not be able to do so. But it may be only one of those gloomy forebodings which torment us sometimes without real foundation, and from which the Lord, if He finds us faithful, delivers us happily; and so may it be with our beloved mother. There will be lip service enough to her when we go; but there are, of all about her, only ourselves upon whom she can depend. O wife! when I think on all she hath been to me since a child, I could give my life for her, even though I were to lose thee, my darling."

"And I would follow thee, my lord. Life would be death without thee; for, besides thee and our mother, whom have I in all the world to protect me against that bad, terrible man, whose last threatening still often seems to ring in my ears?"

A few days more, and through a pass in the Manikdown Hills, they reached the considerable town of Ashtee, and thence Bhatoree, a pretty village lying at the foot of the mountain, which is crowned by the noble mausoleum of Sulabut Khan. There was a comfortable summer palace there, now much decayed, but still habitable, which was then perfect, and the Queen found it ready for her reception. Groves of mango trees around afforded ample shelter for her followers and escort; and the situation was so beautiful that many from Beejapoor, who had expected to find only a savage wilderness of mountains, were now charmed with the prospects before them. One more march, and the Royal city would be gained in safety.

Here, too, all the officers and functionaries of State, with their followers and troops, came to pay their respects and offer their "mezzins" to the Royal lady. And though some had never seen her, yet there were many who remembered her marriage; and by none was the glorious campaign of 1564 forgotten, and all—old or new—were charmed with her grace and dignity, the wisdom of her counsels, and, as far as she could decide them, her own intentions; and she assured all that she should leave them no more until God willed to take her, and exhorted them to be faithful and true. So as soon as the palace in the citadel could be prepared for her, the Queen made a triumphal march into the city and fort.

Outwardly Ahmednugger presents no imposing appearance like Beejapoor. There are no lofty palaces towering over the walls, no tall minarets or domed mosques like those she had left behind her; but the city had an aspect of comfort and peace, and the gardens of the Furhat Mahal, the Bihishtee Bagh, or Garden of Paradise, were inviting and pleasant to view, and though comparatively low, the Royal palace in the fort was full of comfort. The faithful Mullek Umber, governor of Dowlutabad, had sent from his new capital, Kirkee, large baskets full of oranges and delicious grapes, writing that in the course of a few days he would come himself; and there was no person whom the Queen more earnestly desired to see, or in whom she reposed higher confidence. Mullek Umber was, indeed, a remarkable man. From the condition of an Abyssinian eunuch he had raised himself to the rank of a viceroy of the kingdom, and governor of one of the largest provinces of the Ahmednugger dominions. He had—following the example of the Emperor Akhbar—surveyed and assessed all the lands in every village of the country, and reduced the whole to a system which operated most beneficially to the State as well as to the people. To this day the original settlements exist in many a village record, and are proof of the skill and patience with which they were executed, requiring little alteration to suit modern demands. A humane, devout man, as well as charitable and just, but not one to be drawn into the intrigues and dissensions of a Court. Whatever happened there, he preserved a dignified neutrality; too strong in his local position, and in the devotion of his numerous troops, to be meddled with by anyone. He had infinite respect for Queen Chand. He had followed the events of her career with profound interest, and he could see that except through her the affairs of the State had little chance of settlement or indeed of salvation from ruin; and he watched with much anxiety what the result of Queen Chand's first acts would be, though his counsel, when asked, was given freely and honourably.

For the first week or more events at Ahmednugger were without excitement, and nothing occurred to disturb their even current. The Queen and her companions made excursions to the Royal palaces and gardens without the fort; and even to one at some little distance, in a ravine of the eastern range of hills, built near a pretty cascade, which is well known to all present inhabitants of the English cantonment as the "Happy Valley." There the broad plain of the Godavery lay out before them; and even the grim rock fort of Dowlutabad, and the tall white minaret of the Emperor Mahomed Toghluk, were distinctly visible on a clear day. Maria and her brother were already longing to proceed thither, and visit the Portuguese who had settled there, many of whom were vine-dressers and orange cultivators; and the Queen promised that when Mullek Umber should arrive she would despatch them with him. Meanwhile, among the gunners and artificers of the local army the Bishop and Maria had found many fellow-Christians; and as no feeling of bigotry appeared to exist against them, they promised themselves much success in their mission work; while some of the Aurungabad Christians came over to partake of the sacraments of the Church, and were heartily welcomed.

Thus passed many weeks. The Queen had received answers to all her despatches. The Dekhany leader had not returned, but remained with the Golconda troops, who were to take up their position at Owsa, while those of Beejapoor occupied Nuldroog. Although some pretenders to support the party of the spurious new King were known to exist, yet for the most part the succession, in the right direct line, by causing the child Prince Bahadur to be crowned, and appointing the Queen Chand formally to be Regent during the boy's minority, as she had been at Beejapoor, was the desire of the majority. And of this course the sage Mullek Umber entirely approved. There was no doubt of the purity of the boy's descent, who, with his mother, had been confined in the fort of Chawund; and when he arrived he was welcomed with joy, and on a given day was crowned King in the great audience hall of the fort, with every demonstration of satisfaction.

There is no doubt, however, that this bloodless revolution gave secret umbrage to many, and some severe measures had to be taken. Ansar Khan, the governor of the fort, was detected in active correspondence with the Prince Moorad, representing the Queen as an abandoned woman; the boy she had adopted as the son of a minion of her own; and that the people, though they dare not complain, were in the last state of discontent; and Ansar Khan being arraigned before the chiefs and nobles, was convicted and suffered death. Secure in her position, the Queen wrote to the Prince Moorad, recapitulating the past, quoting the recantation of the Dekhany leader who had invited him. As a noble and an honoured guest of the son of the great Emperor, whom it behoved to protect an infant minor—he would be welcome, most welcome, and a friendly embassy and escort would be sent to meet him ; but if hostile intentions still filled his mind, and force were resorted to, she was well supported by her neighbours, and had made every preparation to repel what she could not avert by conciliation.

But the cloud afar off only thickened, and became more and more threatening week by week, and the Queen strained every nerve to preserve the fort to the utmost, and prepare for what could not be much longer averted.

## CHAPTER III.

### THE PROGRESS OF THE SIEGE.

THE rainy season had ceased, and operations could now be undertaken without danger of interruption from the weather. For some months past the Prince Moorad Mirza had watched the progress of events at Ahmednugger with the keenest interest; and had the Dekhany leaders been united in regard to the election of the first King, it is probable he would not have sought to disturb it, but would have made his own terms with them. But their withdrawal from their position, the spirited movement of the Queen Dowager in the coronation of Bahadur, the infant King, and the rallying about her of parties who had before been disunited, promised a very formidable coalition for defence. And when, in addition to local unity, it became certain that the very formidable cavalry of Beejapoor and Golconda had taken the field to cover Ahmednugger, the Prince saw it was time, if he was to strike in at all, to do so at once, before the eastern and southern forces could arrive at their purposed destination. He had with him thirty thousand of the flower of the Moghul cavalry, a large body of Rajpoot infantry and artillery, and several of the most celebrated generals of his father's army led different portions of the troops; and the prospect of a campaign in a new country, and with the celebrated cavaliers of the Dekhan, infused the highest spirits into all classes.

Two men had joined the Prince, in whom he had now much confidence. Not long before, as he was hunting, a cavalier, well appointed, and attended by a small body of spearmen, rode up to him, and offered his services for the Dekhan campaign. He and his family had been, he said, in the service of Beejapoor for some generations; but enemies had prevailed against him, and he had left a service in which he could not stay with honour. He knew the whole country of the Dekhan, and most of the leaders of parties, Dekhanies and foreigners, and could direct the Prince to means of success to which he would, with his own people only, remain a stranger.

This brief colloquy had been followed by a private interview, in which Osman Beg—for it was the man whom we have already seen degraded and dismissed from Beejapoor—laid before the Prince and some of his most esteemed councillors the condition of the whole of the Dekhan, that of its armies and parties, and the position of the Queen Dowager at Ahmednugger, which he did not undervalue. He told them that they should not despise the power of a woman like her, whom no danger could appal, nor ordinary resistance overcome; and that in the Dekhan there was no commander to equal her in the field; while the people loved her, and would, most of them, support her to the last. The great object, therefore, should be to shut her up in Ahmednugger before she could withdraw the infant King to the protection of Beejapoor, which had ample means for defence.

"And what, sir, may be your motive for offering your services to me?" asked the Prince, doubtingly.

"Revenge," returned the other. "Ask me not for what; that may appear in time even to thee. And, for the rest, accept this poor sword, or reject it, as seems best to your Highness. To serve in the army of the King of kings, under his famous son, has long been a dream of mine, wherever that service might lead me. And now that it turns upon my enemies, can I refuse? If my star is not fortunate to gain a place under your Highness, I will seek my fortune elsewhere. I am a soldier, and know no occupation other than my sword gives me."

"Such men are among the necessities of war," said the Prince to Khan Khanan, his commander-in-chief, when they were alone. "What think you of him?"

"I see deceit and treachery in his face," was the reply. "But what can that signify to us? He has some scheme of private revenge to carry out, and he will be faithful to that if not to us. Give him a command, for he has undoubted knowledge of the country which no one else possesses, and in this he will be of use."

So Osman Beg was attached to the division of Khan Jehan, and accompanied the army in the capacity of guide and director of the marches towards Ahmednugger.

Meanwhile Dom Diego had not been idle. Acting under the advice of his banker at Surat, he had written a petition to the Prince, representing himself as a soldier of fortune, recently arrived from Europe, who had knowledge of the attack and defence of fortified places, and the direction of artillery in the field; and, anxious for employment, offered his services to the Royal army. While at Surat he had heard from his cousin at Goa of the appointment of Francis d'Almeida as Bishop of Ahmednugger, and subsequently, that he and his sister had accompanied Queen Chand to her destination. What better opportunity could be afforded for carrying off Maria than the turmoil of a siege and assault. He had seen much service as a soldier in the East. Personally he was brave, and in his own land had studied for the profession of artillery and fortifications. There was no doubt as to his probable usefulness. European adventurers had often rendered very essential service to the Royal armies; but the best of them were at Dehli, and should the applicant be what he described himself, his presence against one of the most celebrated forts of the Dekhan, improved, it was said, by the Portuguese, would be invaluable.

A few days after this, Dom Diego, accompanied by Pedro di Diaz and a party of his sailors accustomed to the use of large guns, arrived in the Royal camp, and was heartily welcomed. The fine martial figure of the new comer made a favourable impression upon the Prince; and the complete suit of mail in which he made his entry into camp, seated on a noble Kattiwar charger, was remarkable and imposing. As before, Pedro di Diaz was his interpreter, but he found the Prince to possess a considerable knowledge of Portuguese, which he had learned at his father's, the Emperor's Court; and Dom Diego, after a short interview, found himself not only much more at his ease than he had expected to be, but appointed to a lucrative post, as inspector and regulator of the artillery.

As he was leaving the Prince's tent, an officer, apparently of the Royal army, came up to him and said, "I ought to know that face. Hast thou forgotten the mission of Moodgul and the plan of Eyn-ool-Moolk?"

"No; thou art Osman Beg," was the reply, "and I have not forgotten. But thou here, my friend? Methought the fair Zóra, whom thou used to tell me about, would have more charms for thee than war?"

"What has brought thee, O friend," returned the other, "has brought me, strange as it is. There are two women in Ahmednugger whom we would have. Nay, deny it not; and we may easily take them when there is none to defend them. Your Maria is there; and what matter if you appear as a soldier to gain her?"

"Thou hast guessed shrewdly, friend," was the reply; "it is even so. I find my life dull without her, and such devotion as I offer to her may be accepted at last. And if not—well, we shall see. I have no relish for priestly offices, and war and its excitement suit me much better. Will the Queen fight?"

"As far as a woman can, she undoubtedly will fight. Men may feel fear, but she does not even in the face of imminent danger. If the people with her are only true to her, you will see that the result will flutter some of these silken love-birds of Dehli. Our Dekhan ways are rough, but the men of Ahmednugger are roughest of all; and some of thy countrymen made the fort what it is."

"Then it will require one of them to open the casket. Who knows where to find the key? And if my old knowledge has not departed from me, I may be able to do what force cannot do, or these wretched guns which the Prince thinks so much of."

"And the guns of Ahmednugger foundries have ever been famous since the days of Chuleby Roomy Khan, the Turk, and many have been bought from your countrymen. I would advise caution, Señor; and may Alla send us a good deliverance! When the time comes, we may be able to help each other; till then we may meet seldom, or not at all, for my place will be the advanced division."

"And mine with the main body and the Prince, where you will always find me, Osman Beg, at your service. If you will keep your own counsel, I can keep mine; and though we care for what we hope to win, there are many here who would laugh at us if they knew our desires; and, from what I hear, the Prince sets his face against any abduction of the enemy's women."

"I, at least, can demand my wife, after the custom of our law," said Osman Beg, with a swagger.

"When she is the wife of another? Ha! ha!" returned the priest, with a sneering laugh. "You are not particular, perhaps, though I am. But we need not interfere with each other; and so, farewell!"

While the great army was in slow but certain progress towards the goal of its desire, we must return for a brief while to the personages in this tale whom we left there. Since the coronation of the boy King, Bahadur, there had been no violent disturbance of the public peace; and though some of the leaders of parties still held aloof, watching the course of events, others had frankly joined the Queen and declared for her policy. The fort was now full of men, and one of the best soldiers of the State, Nihung Khan, who had been confined at Dowlutabad for several years, was released by Mullek Umber, and sent, with six thousand good cavalry, to keep the frontier, and, if necessary, to join the Queen. The Queen herself, with calm fortitude, collected provisions till the fort granaries were quite full. Every piece of ordnance was thoroughly inspected, and made fit for service. Shot, powder, entrenching tools, and gabions were prepared; nor, in consultation with her artillery officers, was any measure left incomplete for defence. All walls, huts, and some houses which had encroached upon the esplanade were levelled, and nothing existed to obstruct the fire of the place. She was fearful of exciting jealousy in the minds of her troops, and did not therefore appoint Abbas Khan to the command of the fort, as she wished to do; but he was her indefatigable assistant in every department; nor was there a day in which the Royal lady did not visit works in progress, or go out on visits of inspection to points where it was suggested trenches might be made, or other hindrances to the enemy's advance contrived.

There continued, however, one permanent source of disquietude and anxiety to her, which was the inactivity of the Beejapoor and Golconda forces, for as yet they had made no forward movement; and as the weather was now open, they ought to have taken up the positions she had suggested. Once, indeed, when she wrote to Soheil Khan, the Beejapoor officer in command, that the Moghul cavalry were about to make a movement to turn the flank of the general defences of the kingdom, twelve thousand cavalry were despatched from Nuldroog, by way of Bheer, to hold hem in check; but the movement proved futile, the Beejapoor force was defeated and routed by six thousand Moghuls, under Khan Jehan Lody, one of the best generals of the army, and the Beejapoor troops fled back from the Godavery in confusion, to tell tales of Moghul prowess, which considerably added to the existing alarm. In truth, Osman Beg had rendered essential service in this movement. By a rapid march he had turned the flank of the forces which covered Dowlutabad; he had prevented the junction of Nihung Khan's troops with those of Beejapoor; and by the defeat of the latter, the rear of Ahmednugger, the fertile plain of the Godavery, and several easy passes up to the very precincts of the fort, were left in almost perfect tranquillity to the invaders. Thenceforth the Queen knew she had no one from whom she could expect aid, but she did not relax her preparations or her vigilance. She knew her nephew could not leave Beejapoor, for without one or other of them the capital could not be trusted; and Soheil Khan, the general who had been sent with the cavalry, though a brave man, was by no means an enterprising officer, or one on whom she could depend in an emergency. Oh! that it had been Humeed Khan, or anyone of the devoted friends who had ever supported her, then there would have been neither doubt nor hesitation. Soheil Khan was a calm, reflective man, and it was on this account, perhaps, that he had been sent. He could perceive clearly enough that if Beejapoor took any open part in the war, the Moghuls, when Ahmednugger fell, would infallibly declare war against it, and that, under all considerations, would be the safest policy.

At first, our friends the Bishop and his sister had thought that peace would not be broken. The Queen seemed so firm in her position, the fort was so strong, and the enemy so distant, that Francis d'Almeida did not like to defer taking up the charge he was responsible for to his Church; and, taking advantage of the arrival of Mullek Umber, they travelled in his suite on his return; but they found only comparatively very few Christians at Dowlutabad, who were cultivators of grapes and oranges, and a few at the new city of Kirkee, which was then being built—who were gunners and soldiers. Many years before, a lay monk had settled among them from Goa, and had contrived to keep the little flock together; but both Francis and Maria saw that it could not readily increase, and that it would be a waste of time to remain there longer than would be necessary to establish the foundations of what might arise hereafter; and when a small chapel in the city of Kirkee was completed under Mullek Umber's assistance, who, it was believed, had greater reverence for his old faith than was consistent with his profession of Islam, they took their departure, and arrived at Ahmednugger shortly before the irruption of the Moghuls and the defeat of the Beejapoor forces had closed the valley of the Godavery to general travellers.

The Queen was rejoiced at her friends' arrival. If for a brief time she had doubted whether the comparative quiet and security of Dowlutabad would not prove more attractive to them than the imminent risk of war which menaced her, their arrival dispelled all such thoughts, and she estimated at its full worth the devotion and good faith of the Bishop and his sister. They had not only returned to their flock, but were prepared to render such assistance as their peaceful calling enabled them to do very usefully and practically. As there was no apparent chance of being relieved by Beejapoor, and an attack by the Moghul army appeared more and more imminent every day, from the reports of progress by the enemy, the worthy Bishop set himself to organise something in the form of a hospital, in which Maria, from former experience at Goa, was able to render her brother very essential service. A large magazine was cleared out, and fitted as well as circumstances would allow for the purpose. Bandages, splints, and such other necessaries as could be obtained, were stored in it; and while the result was watched curiously by the garrison, yet it gave assurance in no small degree that the wounded would be cared for, and not left to chance, as was too often the case.

We need not, perhaps, follow the daily routine of lives which had no change, nor any alleviation of anxiety common to all. The Queen held her accustomed durbars, and received reports; she visited the posts as often as was possible, especially at night, to guard against surprise; and with the danger growing nearer and nearer, appeared to display increasing fortitude and resignation, and this demeanour had incited in her garrison the highest spirit of devotion and loyalty. Maria and Zóra, her indefatigable assistants, had their hands full of work of their own ; but at times of comparative leisure they met together, read to or conversed with their Royal mistress, or often in the still evenings sat with her on the terrace roof of the palace, looking over the wide country, and watching the bodies of troops marching to their posts, or exercising in the open space in the centre of the fort, till the evening watches were set, and all at last was at rest.

If Nihung Khan and his Abyssinians could but arrive, the accession of strength would prove an additional security. But day after day passed, and he came not. There were no means of communicating with him, while messenger after messenger was captured or cut off by the force of Khan Jehan Lody, which seemed to be as ubiquitous as it was vigilant. But the Queen did not abandon hope, she knew Nihung Khan to be wary and vigilant, and should he confine himself to the duty of harassing the besiegers and cutting off their supplies, important services would be rendered.

And at last no doubt remained. On December 12, according to the local history, the leading troops of the Moghuls advanced within sight of the fortress. All the morning their kettle-drums and trumpets had been heard in the distance, and by a little after noon the crowd of officers, of cavalry, with the Prince's royal canopy in the centre, borne upon a lofty elephant, appeared in the vicinity of the Hushti Bihisht Gardens, which had been the scene of many a pleasant day's festival for the Queen and her companions. It was in vain that Abbas Khan, and spirited young leaders like himself, pressed her to allow them to make a sally and endeavour to throw the enemy into confusion; the Queen positively forbade the attempt. If Nihung Khan did appear, they might advance to assist him; but any reverse now would make her situation more desperate, and render the defence of the fort—in which she, perhaps, placed too much confidence—out of the question altogether.

Early next morning they watched the great army form in line—a magnificent though terrible spectacle—and the Royal Prince, accompanied by some officers, rode round the fort, out of reach of shots, pointing out to the leaders of each division the ground it was to occupy. One officer, who acted more boldly than the rest, advanced near enough to be within reach of shot, but escaped unhurt. As they all watched him from the roof of the palace, Abbas Khan felt sure he was a European; but the Royal army contained many such adventurers, and the Bishop, though he could not distinguish the features, felt a conviction that it could be no other than Dom Diego. He, however, kept his own counsel, and said nothing to his sister.

During that day and part of the next the investiture of the fort was completed on three sides—north, west, and south; but the east side was not closed. Now Nihung Khan, whose advance had been so eagerly looked for, had made a rapid march to Beejapoor, and had represented to the King Ibrahim the extreme danger of the Queen's position. He had succeeded in obtaining some cavalry, which with his own levy made up about seven thousand men; and with this he had hoped to arrive before the fort was invested, but if not, to cut his way through the enemy's lines. He had also, when within twelve miles of the fort, sent out spies, who not only reported to him that the east side was as yet unoccupied, but contrived to inform the Queen that he was at hand, and would, God willing, be with her next day; and we may imagine with what intense anxiety he was expected.

The Queen had arisen before daylight, and was watching with Zóra from their usual place, when they heard suddenly a great but distant clamour arise to the eastward of the fort, which continued for some time. At last a body of horsemen, some few hundreds only in number, emerged from under cover of some hedges, and at headlong speed crossed the esplanade. It was Nihung Khan, who had marched during the night with his whole body, but found that, instead of an open passage to the fort, he became engaged with the Khan Khanan's powerful division of the Royal army. He himself, with his immediate body-guard, had cut his way through the enemy to join his Royal mistress, leaving the main body, which had retreated, to retire upon the Beejapoor forces. Welcome as a gallant soldier like Nihung Khan was, even with a comparative handful of men, yet, on the other hand, there was no longer any doubt that the investiture of the fort was complete, and that the siege had commenced.

The enemy's operations were conducted with skill and military science. No other measures would have been available against such a place as Ahmednugger. Dom Diego, after several feints, established his head-quarters and trenches on the south-west side of the fort, and thence continued his approaches by regular parallels to the crest of the glacis, or as near as possible to the point, whence, eventually, the breaching batteries were established; but the defenders' artillery was infinitely superior to his own, and the operations had been slow and difficult. Not only did the artillerists of the fort maintain their ancient reputation, but the practice of the Arabs in the garrison was very fatal. With their excellent matchlocks nothing could show itself in the Moghul trenches without being hit, and the real terror they inspired was very great. Then the garrison became more and more confident, and their courage rose in proportion. Day and night the Queen herself patrolled the fort, watching the terrible game with a kind of fascination. Nor could her ordinary companions be restrained from sharing the danger with her; while, at night, the well-known slight figures, passing from post to post, were greeted with many a fervent blessing and prayer for their safety. And who shall tell of the gentle ministrations of Maria and her brother; the care and skill with which wounds were dressed; the soothing and thirst-assuaging drinks that were composed and ministered? Sometimes the worthy Bishop would accompany Meeah in his rounds, or sit with him at his post, offering a hint here, a suggestion there, as far as his small military skill enabled him to do; and when the point of attack was finally established, his directions as to the flanking fire to be maintained, in case any breach was made, were eminently useful. "Priests," he said one day, laughing, "need not be soldiers; yet in my country many a Bishop has been obliged to fight for the cause of his Church, and why not I for my little flock?" Thus, in the semi-circular bastion at the angle, which was large and roomy, and held a number of guns, he succeeded in placing two of the best pieces in the fort; and for the defence and the cover of the gunners he used large gabions filled with earth, which afforded complete protection. It was in vain that Dom Diego directed his guns upon this and other large bastions defended in the same manner. The nearer he approached, the more deadly was the defenders' fire. His trenches were raked by it, and by no means could it be silenced. Nor were the Ahmednugger gunners forgetful of the legend of the employment of bags of the heavy square copper money of the country, and occasionally a shower of it was sent hurtling through the air with a screaming noise which inspired more terror, perhaps, than it did actual mischief, except at very close quarters.

In truth, Dom Diego's position was not an enviable one. The Prince had looked to him to discover some easy manner in which the fort might be at once assaulted and taken by storm. Any sacrifice of men he would have considered of no consequence; but the admirable construction of Ahmednugger forbade any attempt at escalade with hope of success. Its lofty walls, its deep and extremely broad ditch, the height of the counterscarp and defences for musketry were unapproachable. The Moghul artillery, too, was none of the best, and was too light for siege purposes; very little effect had been produced upon the lower part of the fort. Here and there a few stones had been broken and displaced, but the facing only covered and marked the real strength which was in the earth, solidified by age, of which the rampart was composed. Day after day guns melted at the vent or at the muzzle, and became useless, and no progress was made.

On the part of the commanders of the Royal army, two anxieties of a very serious character were ever present. Provisions were getting very scarce, scarce enough to reduce the ordinary rations of the men and horses. For although the Beejapoor troops did not advance to the capital, they had command of the most fertile districts, from which grain and forage could be derived; and the circle grew narrower. This, however, was kept a profound secret, and the operations were continued as usual.

The beginning of February had now arrived, and progress in the siege was as dilatory as ever; and at a council of war the whole chances of success were discussed calmly. Should the Beejapoor troops advance, the siege must be raised; and in regard to the siege itself all seemed to depend upon the success of mining, which Dom Diego had counselled from the first, but which the native excavators declared to be impossible on account of the firm, stony nature of the soil. If mines could be carried under even one of the central bastions, and a breach made, there would, it was considered, be no doubt of success.

Just then the Queen wrote in the most urgent terms she could to the Beejapoor officers. If they advanced at once, and operated against the rear of the Moghul lines, nothing could save the enemy from defeat, and most likely destruction, for their cattle were already dying of starvation; the fort was still intact, and there had been but few casualties; in short, that victory was within their grasp if they would but take it. These letters were intercepted by Osman Beg, who took them to the Prince, who added a few lines of his own in a chivalrous spirit, to the effect that he had marched from Dehli on purpose to cross swords with the cavaliers of the

Dekhan, and was waiting for them, and trusted they would not delay the opportunity he had so long desired.

But no result followed on these letters, and the Queen almost began to despair of the good faith of Beejapoor. Why should they allow such an opportunity to escape? Again and again did Abbas Khan and Nihung Khan press her to allow them to depart secretly and make their way through the hills ; but the Royal lady felt that the danger to the fort must draw to a head, and whether the Moghuls raised the siege and departed, or whether the crisis of an assault arrived, their presence was alike indispensable.

## CHAPTER IV.

### THE ASSAULT.

FOR several days the fire of the besiegers had much slackened, and the spirits of the besieged rose in proportion to the highest pitch. Were the Moghuls in reality preparing to abandon the attack and retire? It might be so, indeed, for a considerable body of Beejapoor cavalry had at last moved forwards and taken post in the Manikdown Hills, from whence their operations against the Moghul supplies and distant outposts were beginning to be seriously felt; but they were by no means strong enough to effect any considerable diversion, and, up to the night of Feb. 20, affairs continued in the same position. But the inactivity of the enemy appeared unaccountable to the Queen and her council. Upon what could they be relying? The allied armies were at Bheer, and by a sudden and energetic march might be with her in three days; but it was impossible for the Queen to communicate with her friends, every egress from the fort being so vigilantly watched night and day. But the suspense only lasted till the night of the day we have named, when, as all were watching on the walls, a loud manly voice was heard from the opposite side of the ditch, which cried out—

"O ye brave friends and brothers in the faith, no longer make a vain resistance. Ye have fought well for your honour, and may save the shedding of more blood. Under the five bastions whereon ye stand five mines have been silently driven. They are loaded and ready, and they will be fired to admit the army of the King of kings. Beware, then, for I have warned ye; and your fate cannot be averted but by surrender."

Then, amidst the profoundest silence, the voice ceased. No figure was seen, for it was a profoundly dark night, and some, overcome with awe, cried, "It is a warning from the Lord; it is the voice of an angel; who shall resist it?" and a great fear fell upon all. But the strange incident only seemed to inspire the heroic Queen with new courage, and mounting a slight elevation of the parapet, her clear, sweet voice was heard above all murmurs.

"Shall we who are unhurt, and have victory in our grasp if we persevere, give up our swords, and like frightened women betake ourselves to the feet of the invader and beg for our lives? Shall we, with arms in our hands, cease to use them to protect all dear to us. Your women and children, O my sons, will hardly thank ye for abandoning them to the brutal violence of the Moghul soldiers. Behold! I am but a woman, and a weak one; but I leave not this spot with my life; and, come what may, I rely upon the most just Lord to deliver us and ye all from this tyranny. Away, bring up the miners; we know the places, so there is no doubt. Bring tools, and set to work. I would rather tear up the earth with my weak fingers, than suffer this danger to exist while we have the time and the means to avert it."

Then arose a hoarse cry of "We will not desert thee, O Mother. We will die if it be God's will, but we will not yield. Fear not then, but see what we do."

At first there was some little confusion, but gangs were speedily organised, and with a hearty good will they set to work, led by the Queen, who, with a pickaxe in her hand, descended into the shaft, and, with those dearest to her about her, worked like the rest; going from shaft to shaft, distributing draughts of cool water and sherbet to those who suffered thirst. It was impossible to exceed the enthusiasm which her heroism inspired.

Nihung Khan, Abbas Khan, and even the pacific Bishop, excited by the turmoil, ran from place to place and encouraged all. Nor was the result disappointing. While they were thus employed, another voice called to them from the bottom of the wall to surrender, for that at daylight the mines would be sprung. But the warning passed unheeded; two mines had been laid bare, and the charges of powder removed after sharp contests under ground; and the Queen was in the act of distributing rewards for the removal of the charge of a third, when, with a fearful report and crash, a fourth mine, as yet undiscovered, was sprung just as day dawned on the scene, and a few yards of the wall fell.

When the first mine had been struck by the counterminers, and the persons driven out of it had gained the trenches, the alarm was at once given in the camp, and the Prince Moorad hurried to the spot at a moment of extreme peril to the Moghul army, for the first mines had occupied the better part of a month. But the skill of the counterminers was so evident from the rapidity with which they had discovered and disarmed them during the night, that it seemed hopeless to continue the work, as well on account of the nature of the ground as because provisions were on the point of exhaustion. His adviser, Dom Diego, had not foreseen such a catastrophe as failure. He had visited the mines the evening before while they were being charged ; he had watched the skill with which the native miners laid the charges and tamped them ; and the result would, he thought, inevitably be that three at least of the mines must destroy the bastions under which they were placed, and furnish three practicable breaches for the stormers, who would be composed of the flower of the Royal army. But these plans had failed. All that remained was one small mine under a part of the curtain, which had been intended to enlarge another of the main mines. It might make a practicable breach, but it would be a narrow one, and it might possibly fail altogether.

The Prince and Dom Diego stood together on one of the parapets of the temple looking over the fort, the interior of which, as the day was breaking, could be seen distinctly, with the thousands of men like ants hurrying to and fro, carrying earth in baskets, in cloths, and as best they could, from the countermines. Parties of them were collecting, and even breaking the surface of the ground near the small mine we have mentioned. Dom Diego pointed out the place to the Prince.

"There is our last resource, for the other mines are not charged; and they would be useless if they were. Shall I fire it? We shall at least see what sort of a heap it makes; and I, for one, am ready to lead any party your Highness may appoint to storm it."

"Well said, sir," exclaimed the Prince, "and like a gallant soldier. When thou art within thou wilt have the treasury and Royal jewels to help thyself from, and I hear they are both rich."

"My treasure is of another kind," replied Diego, "and I do not intend to neglect it. Shall the mine be fired?"

"Bismilla!" cried the Prince. "Lose no time."

"I have laid the train," said Pedro di Diaz, who came up at the instant; "but the chamber is not half charged, not enough tamped, but it will do something."

"Then fire it in the devil's name," cried Dom Diego. "I will watch."

A few moments more, and two thin columns of smoke issued from the fort wall, and from that part of the counterscarp which was opposite. These places heaved slightly upwards, and earth and stones arose with a muffled sound, casting into the air the bodies of a number of men who had been walking on the fort wall. The effect of these explosions was a clear road into the ditch from the counterscarps, and an apparently practicable though steep breach in the rampart of the fort.

"It is done!" cried Dom Diego, with a wave of his plumed hat to the Prince. "If your Highness will send for the stormers I will lead them at once, if they will follow me."

In the fort, as the smoke and dust of the explosion cleared away, some of the garrison seemed to have given up hope, and were girding their loins for flight; but the Queen was equal to the emergency. While she called to those about her to remember their oath to her, to rally their men, for the gates were closed, and there was no egress for flight, she cried, "And whither would ye fly, O sons and brothers? To the plain yonder, to perish by the swords of your enemies? Nay, for your honour's sake, desert me not now; and to the latest day of the Dekhan your deeds shall be sung by bards and minstrels. See, we women blench not from the storm; and she who brings my armour and my sword, a holy Syud's daughter, will die here with me, and her husband, my children both, rather than yield while we have life." Then, as Zóra, clad in the old green dress of the Turreequt, approached, the Queen withdrew for an instant, and putting on her morion and a suit of light chain mail, with gauntlets, and waving a naked sword, came forward among them, crying the old battle cry of her husband. Over her face, as it was becoming light, she had cast a transparent veil, but every feature was visible, glowing with a rapt enthusiasm and confidence.

"To the breach, my friends, with me!" she cried. "Who will follow my veil? Behold it will lead you to honour, if to death; never to infamy. If we die, we shall sip the nectar of Paradise ere night."

No one attempted to resist this appeal. With passionate cries of devotion, with tears and sobs, the leaders and men, with her beloved Abbas Khan, pressed forward to do their best in her defence. The rough veteran, Nihung Khan, with tears flowing down his cheeks, besought her to retire to a place of safety, but she cried the more that she would remain; and in her own Battle of the Veil it behoved her to lead, and no other.

But it was yet some time before the Moghuls advanced to storm, and the delay enabled the besiegers to make some defence for the breach available. A double row of gabions was placed over the crest, and filled with earth; the best marksmen among the Arabs and the garrison were posted on the wall above its sides; wall pieces were brought from other parts of the fort; rocket-men plied their rockets on the crest of the glacis opposite, through which a road had been sloped from above. Behind the gabions, and sheltered by them, dense bodies of spearmen stood in serried ranks. In short, no precaution that Abbas Khan and his companions could bethink themselves of was neglected. Even the Bishop, who the whole night through had been at work, ran from his post on the large bastion to see that all was in proper order, and his few directions were practical and useful.

Every preparation had been made that could be contrived. Every gun that the fortifications allowed of had been trained on the breach and the enemy's road thither. The garrison had been divided into bodies, so as to relieve each other as quickly as possible without crowding; and though the enemy fired occasionally from the trenches against the breach and the parapets of walls, the precautions which had been taken of covering the men with gabions and sand-bags almost entirely prevented casualties. As to the breach itself, though the enemy fired continually at it, they produced no effect, as their shot, knocking up a cloud of dust, only sank into the earth harmlessly. Presently, also, Abbas Khan and some of the boldest Arabs contrived to let down some gabions below the crest of the breach, where they established themselves, thus affording increased matchlock fire of a fatal character, besides opposing an additional obstacle to the stormers.

"He is sending us his best soldiers, mother," said Abbas Khan, settling his turban more firmly on his head, as he prepared to descend to his post; "but fear not, none will come near thee."

"Rather let one blow of thy good sword release me, son," she said. "'Twould be but kindness, if God will."

He made no reply; but the tears welled up in his eyes as he left her and his beloved wife together, and heard their cries of "Deen! Deen!" as he entered his perilous position.

Still they waited and no advance was made; and the Queen was not unmindful of the necessity of furnishing food for the men who had watched with her all night. Since very early, before daylight, the cooks had been busy preparing pilaos and boiled meats, which now began to arrive in huge cauldrons, and was distributed to the men by companies; and all sat down and ate their plattersful, or gathered round huge dishes, and ate their fill; but no one moved from his appointed station; while the Queen and her attendants, disdaining more delicate viands prepared for them, partook of the general mess of camels' meat and rice, plentifully seasoned with pepper and onions, and which was by no means to be despised by hungry folk. Indeed, for the time, the area of the fort in the vicinity of the breach was a place of feasting. Elephants moved to and fro with large water-skins, and men bearing jars of cool sherbet gave freely to those that needed it; and, taking example from the Queen's forethought, every private house in the fort sent its quota of food or of drink.

So noon came, and the voice of the muezzin chaunted the call to prayer from different quarters of the fort, as if no deadly strife were imminent, and the Moslems spread scarves or waist-bands where they stood or sat. The Queen had not stirred since the morning from the place she had taken up near the gabions; and the only protection she would allow the people to make for her and Zóra against the sun was a few cloths tied to spears. Once Maria had come to see her from her own post, the hospital, but there was no time for much speaking; and, committing them to the care of God, she returned to her post with her brother, the masses of rough soldiery making way for her with the most profound respect. One look with her brother she took from the great flanking bastion along the side of the fort attacked, and it gave her an assurance she could hardly have expected.

The whole side of the fort was uninjured, except near the breach, where there had been much pelting by the enemy's shot, but no fracture. The *débris* of the mine had spread out as far as the bottom of the ditch, and partly lay on its level floor; but it seemed, even to her, a perilous place for people to ascend. Some part of the counterscarp had apparently been dug down or blown in, and it was evidently the way by which the enemy would approach. All along the wall, every gun that could be aimed was directed upon the breach, and the two beautiful bastions which formed the Queen's post.

One reason for delay was the indecision in the Moghul camp. Many experienced veterans declared that it was waste of life only to attempt to storm Ahmednugger by such a breach as had been made. Reproachful epithets were freely banded about, and it seemed a question whether any attack would be made that day. But Dom Diego's savage temper would brook no control. "I will take the place with the five Europeans I have," he cried, "and cowards can follow at their leisure; as if breaches in fort walls were to be made like beaten highways for dainty fops to strut upon." Dom Diego was, in truth, weary of the idleness of the Moghul officers. There was not a true soldier among them, and he often thought failure imminent; but Maria was there, and while it was possible to win her, even a soldier's death would be better than the hell of tumultuous feeling which raged within him.

At last the signal for assault was given from the enemy's camp. First, the huge imperial kettle-drums sounded a march in their deep booming notes, and a general discharge of all their artillery in the trenches followed; while, in the bastion of the fort, the Portuguese and Hindoo native gunners stood or lounged among their piles of shot and bags of copper coin. Many of them were known to Maria; their wives were helping her in her own work, and all saluted her reverently and affectionately as she left them with a prayer that the Lord would protect them all.

All through the Moghul trenches the silence was almost oppressive. The muezzin's call to prayer was proclaimed like that in the fort; and, for a brief space, only a distant hum from the town and camp could be heard. As Maria stood on the steps of the great bastion, she could hear flies buzzing about her, the birds chirruping in the trees near her, and even the lowing and bleating of the cattle and sheep which were grazing in the broad ditch on the sheltered side of the fortress. The sun shone through the thunderous air with a fierce hot glare over all, and the plain and glacis were quivering in the trembling light. The wind had fallen, and the stillness and heat were so oppressive that she was glad to gain the cool shelter of the large vaulted building. Many fresh guns that had been brought to bear upon the breach aroused the echoes even of the distant hills; but the shot had little effect upon the extemporised defences of the breach, or upon the parapets anywhere; and the Queen and Zóra, looking through a loophole that commanded the breach, saw, with a thrill of delight, that Abbas Khan in his perilous post was safe.

Suddenly, on the crest of one of the trenches beyond, a tall, powerful figure, dressed in European costume, stood forth, waving a naked sword, which flashed in the sun; while with the other hand he removed a plumed morion from his head, and made a courteous salute to the fort. He wore a bright corselet of steel, with gauntlets, and a buff coat and boots, richly embroidered. In his left hand he carried a stout stick, but no shield or other defence whatever. For an instant there was a shout of "Shabash!

Shabash Feringi!" and, instantly, a crowd of men scrambled over the trenches, and, as he pointed to the breach, followed him. And these, some hundreds in number, Europeans and native volunteers, formed the forlorn hope. Again, others came on in denser array: Arabs, Pathans, Afghans, Rajpoots, dressed in yellow tunics; and other tribes, many singing their war song, others shouting their national war cries, armed with matchlocks, sword, shield, and spear, flashing in the afternoon sun, which poured its hot rays on all. It was now somewhat past four in the afternoon, and the sultry heat of the day had become almost sickening, when a slight breeze from the west waved the banners of the advancing host, and slightly displaced the cloud of dust which had arisen over them. It was a glorious, awe-inspiring spectacle truly; but the defenders blenched not from it; every man grasped his weapon more firmly, and stood at his post prepared for the worst, should it come. On the far side of the ditch, along the crest of the counterscarp and covered way, clouds of skirmishers spread themselves, pouring their shot upon the defences; but the fire had little effect, and gradually slackened.

Scrambling down the road prepared for them by the mine, and without order, large bodies of stormers now poured across the ditch, the tall figure of the European bounding before them all to the very foot of the breach, when suddenly one of the large guns on each of the flanking bastions sent its deadly discharge of round shot and copper hail among the crowds beneath with fearful effect. Hundreds fell, writhing; while from every bastion rockets, fire-balls, and musketry smote them as they lay or straggled onwards. There was no chance of retreat, for the masses in the rear, which came on in a continuous stream, were not checked, and any of the foremost who faltered, or turned to fly, were thrown down and trampled into the dust. Again and again did Dom Diego attempt the breach, but the earth was so loose that footing could hardly be maintained; and the grim serried ranks which covered the crest of the breach gave little hope that could he and those with him reach the bristling ranks of broad spears beyond, they could force an entrance, while Abbas Khan and his body of Arabs plied them with shot, few of which missed their mark.

But still none of the stormers turned; on the contrary, thousands of men charged down the counterscarp, to be met with the same volleys from the great guns, which proved so deadly and so effective. Once Dom Diego and some hundreds of men, collected hastily, made a rush up the breach, and interchanged blows with its defenders; and Abbas Khan, struck with his devoted bravery, called to him to take quarter, and come to his post; but the humane effort was rejected with an oath, and he fell back among the struggling masses to seek volunteers for a task which was beyond the power of man.

Can we, even in imagination, realise in any degree that fearful maddening scene—the discharges of the great guns at intervals carrying destruction to hundreds at every shot, assisted by the rockets, the musketry, and the fire-balls from the walls? Even these were little in comparison with the frantic struggles of the masses as they were urged on by the Prince in person and his generals—the shouts, the screams, and cries of wounded and dying men, the fierce thirst which consumed all! The ditch, from the first almost covered by the dead and dying, was now rising under the heaps beneath, which every moment augmented. There was no escape and no progress; the masses contrived to descend, ignorant of what was before them; and as it was industriously circulated by the Prince and his advisers that the breach had been stormed and the fort was being plundered all rushed on to gain a share of the riches it was supposed to contain—only to be met by the withering fire which destroyed them, and the horrible heaps of carnage grew higher and higher as the evening wore on.

As to Queen Chand, we read in the old chronicles how—fearless among the storm of shot, dauntless among the horrid cries and shrieks which filled the air—she was seen everywhere, distributing rewards, giving water to the wounded and thirsty, and encouraging all. Nor was the green figure beside her less active or less useful. Sometimes they were at the breach, down which they looked, with a fascination which could not be repressed, upon the masses of struggling forms beneath them. But still Zóra saw her brave lord safe; and he even smiled and waved them back, as the Queen, mounting the parapet of the gabions, spoke a few words of encouragement to their defenders. All saw her as she defended the breach in person; and the flutter of the "standard of the veil," which she still wore over her bright morion, was watched by many an one of the enemy's officers, and even by the Prince himself, with unqualified admiration of her heroism.

At last night began to fall, and here and there a star peeped out from the pure ether through the thick, heated vapour from the combatants which filled the air; and the baffled Moghuls, leaving their heaps of slain as they were, retired beyond the crest of the counterscarp into their own lines. They had lost thousands, for the ditch was a mass of carcasses which no one could reckon; they had lost arms, standards, officers, and, above all, reputation. That the hosts of the King of kings should have been repulsed from a Dekhan fortress commanded by a woman was a result which none had anticipated, much less the haughty Imperial Prince who had urged on his devoted troops to destruction. Gradually, those that remained of the invaders retreated up the slope, harassed to the last by the rain of copper hail with which they had been tormented; and the Queen and Zóra, with some of the bravest of the women and eunuchs, watched the last retreating figures which staggered up the slope beyond; or a man here and there extricating himself from the horrible masses like one rising from the dead, followed them alone, or sank down and perished with the rest. And then, as if seeing each other for the first time during the fearful day, they cast themselves upon each others' necks and wept for joy. Then, too, Abbas Khan came up from his post bearing in his hand a standard he had taken from an Afghan, who was almost the only man who had reached the little fort. "He was a brave fellow, mother, and would take no quarter, and there was little time for thought; but he died like a brave man under my weapon, and departed to Paradise. O Mother! what can we render to the Lord for these mercies? for ye are unharmed, both of ye."

"Yes," said the Queen, with her eyes overflowing, "thousands and thousands lie yonder dead and dying; but we are safe, and have lost but few; and the good Padré and Maria tend those who suffer."

"If I may, I will go and see Maria," said Zóra, timidly. What would she not have given to fall into her husband's arms and weep out her thankfulness, but that was not the time or place.

"Go, child," said the Queen. "Go! greet her from me, and say all is safe and well; but do not let her see that," and she pointed to the ditch, "it might appal her tender nature." And

Zóra went, attended by Yasin Khan and some others to fulfil her tender mission, and gain relief for her overcharged mind.

"And now," said the Queen to Abbas Khan and those near him, "let us leave nothing undone. The breach has, indeed, been saved; but it must be made sure. I, for one, will not leave it till it is built up against any chance of surprise, or even of attack. Do not talk to me of sleep or rest. My best sleep would be here beside the workers. My best rest can only come with security. Ye will see what endurance this weak body hath when danger is present. It is an old employment of mine repairing breaches; but at Beejapoor I worked three days and nights without sleep and here, with so many men, all should be ready by daylight; and then when the Moghuls see their labour has been in vain, they may leave us in peace. See and get Zóra some food and rest," she whispered to Abbas Khan, "she will need it."

"Not while thou art here, O Mother," was the reply. "She is young and strong, and can bear it better than thou. But why remain? Canst thou not trust Nihung Khan and myself to do all?"

"No!" she replied, firmly; "it is my work and I will do it. Nor shall Zóra leave me; she will be better for seeing Maria. But my turn has not yet come. Hark! there is a cry from the heap of dead. 'For the love of God! for the love of God! water!' it cries. Does no one hear? It is some Feringi."

"It may be the cavalier who led the assault," said Abbas Khan. "I saw him sink down, but he may have survived."

"A gallant fellow," said the Queen. "I, too, watched him. Go, one of ye, for the Padré Sahib; tell him to come with his bandages and medicine. Quick! quick!"

Abbas Khan, and some men with blankets, descended the breach to the foot, but among the dead on the slope they could find no one living. They dare not take a torch for fear of drawing upon them fire from the counterscarp. They listened, and at last the faint cry of "Aqua! Aqua!" was repeated, but in a fainter tone.

"He is here," cried one of the men, "lying under others, and he is warm. I see his face now; it is the Feringi."

The Queen was right. Her quick ears had heard a low cry in a strange accent, which had escaped all others around her. It was from Dom Diego, who, as we know, had led the forlorn hope. When the mines had been sprung, he would have advanced at once under the cover of the smoke and dust which hung over the wall and ditch, but he found to his vexation that the men were not ready. The hour was not propitious, and the Court astrologer could not discover a fitting time till the afternoon. No one would follow him till the signal was given from the Royal pavilion. And though Dom Diego cursed the delay, he had no alternative but to await the general order, which came at length.

Dom Diego had done his part bravely. He had led three separate assaults of the breach, but was as yet unwounded. Nor was his example lost on the brave men who, as one party was beaten back, or sank down to make a fresh portion of the horrible bridge, still formed afresh, and, reinforced by others crowding on from behind, were led only to perish in their turn. At last, in one of the desperate rushes up the breach, Dom Diego fell from a matchlock shot, but for a moment only. He rose to his feet, and strove to rally those with him, when his leg was shattered by a round shot, and in the discharge of copper hail which came with it, his left arm was broken, and he fell insensible among the heap of dying and dead, and was trampled down with the rest. Presently, however, his consciousness returned; but it only revealed to him more certainly the hopelessness of his situation. Extrication from the mass of dead and dying was impossible, and he must die—unshriven, and without hope. We dare not follow his thoughts nor his cries, now defiant, now despairing, nor the struggles of a Christian soul which, believing in the hell which seemed opening before him, saw no hope of repentance or forgiveness. At first it was beyond his power to move; but several men above him in their death agonies had loosened the pile he lay under, and with his right arm he had been able to push aside the dead who most oppressed him, and thus he gained space to breathe. It was, however, but a prolongation of his misery, for he felt that his leg was shattered, and even to crawl, could he be freed, would be impossible. He could see the forms of men on the ramparts and in the breach moving about, and even hear them as they spoke one to another; but his cries for help and for water had grown fainter and fainter till the Queen's ear had distinguished them.

Then Abbas Khan, and the rest who had gone down the breach, lifted away the dead from above him and raised him up, placing him in a blanket, and carried him up into the fort. At the top they laid him down at the foot of the Bishop, who anxiously looked at the face of the sufferer, who was now insensible.

"Merciful God!" he cried, lifting up his hands to heaven; "it is Dom Diego, and he still lives! Bring him to the rest of the wounded. Quick, quick!" he continued, to Abbas Khan, "or he may die without help."

## CHAPTER V.

### DIEGO'S DEATH AND THE BISHOP'S EMBASSY.

THEY carried the wounded man gently in the blanket as he lay. It was impossible to attempt a palanquin, as the motion would have caused him additional agony. But he was now more sensible than at first. He had drunk greedily from a cup of the Queen's own cool sherbet, which she had kindly sent him; water had been plenteously sprinkled on his face and hands by the Bishop; his pulse had somewhat rallied, and he was even endeavouring to speak, but was forbidden. "Maria! forgive!" were the only words he could utter. Thus they took him on, nor was it far to the place. There were lamps lighted inside, and wounded men lying on mattresses on the floor; and some, which were the worst cases, upon small truckle beds; and on one of these they placed the dying man, supporting him by pillows. There were several Portuguese soldiers there also, who were tending wounded comrades, and all gathered round to assist. Then they carefully unfastened the morion and steel corselet, took off the heavy boots, and the coat of buff leather soaked in blood; and the Bishop supplied some soft underlinen from his own stock with which to dress the wounds. But this seemed hopeless, for several were fatal in their nature, and the loss of blood had been enormous. Maria had been busy at the other end of the wide, long room, and had not seen the new comer; but her brother sent word to her not to come till he sent for her, as the sight would be too shocking. All that she had heard was that the sufferer was a Portuguese officer, and she knew there were some such men in the Prince's army.

D'Almeida's cordial, which had been administered at once, had revived the sinking man in some degree, and for the first time he opened his eyes and stared vacantly about him. Some of the men were bathing his wounds, and this, and the removal of his armour and heavy clothes, had somewhat restored him. Francis d'Almeida was bandaging one of the wounds, which was bleeding afresh, and Dom Diego recognised him, and, with a wan smile, put away his hand and said faintly,—

"It is of no use, brother Francis, I bleed within me, and I am dying. Hear my confession, which I will make to thee truly as long as I can speak; and then let me die."

"It is, indeed, needful, my poor brother," said the Bishop, gently, "for no man living could help thee now, and a brief time must close all thy earthly sufferings. Take this cordial, and it will revive thee. Is there aught that should be written?"

"Something," he said; "that my wealth may be secured to the

Church. But write quickly, or I faint. Can masses be said for my soul, that I may be forgiven? The writing should be in Persian, for the banker at Surat to read."

Who could write Persian there except himself? But the Bishop had seen Zóra with his sister, and he sent word to her to come to him, but not to bring Maria. And she came. A sheet had been spread over the sufferer, and his ghastly wounds were not apparent.

Writing materials were at hand, and seating herself by the bed-side, the girl looked up with a scared face, and asked what she was to write, while Francis interpreted the words as they dropped slowly from his patient's mouth.

"Write," he said, "to Hemchund Premchund, banker of Surat, 'I am dying, my friend, and I will that all my effects in your charge be made over to the illustrious Archbishop of Goa, or whoever he may depute to receive them. Pedro di Diaz is dead, and all there is belongs to me. The ship is to be sold, and the crew paid their wages. Five thousand rupees are to be remitted to my brother, Francis d'Almeida, of this place, for the use of his Church. I am in my full senses, and have this written in Persian that thou mayest comprehend. Be faithful, and discharge thy trust honestly.'"

Zóra's rapid pen soon traced these words, and it was put into Dom Diego's hand by the Bishop. "It is complete," he said; "sign it."

For an instant the dying man rallied, passed his hands across his eyes, and then, taking the pen, wrote in his bold hand,

"D. DIEGO DI FONSECA, S.J.

"My own writing.

"Written at Ahmednugger by Zóra, the wife of Abbas Khan.

"Witness, Francis d'Almeida, Bishop of Ahmednugger, &c. Before us, 3rd Rujub, A.H. 1004, 22nd February, 1596."

"That will do, my brave child," said the Bishop, patting Zóra on the head. "Go back to Maria, and tell her I will send for her soon." And Zóra rose, ran quickly to Maria, and delivered her message.

"Who can he be?" she asked. "Didst thou see his face?"

"I dared not look," Zóra said; "he was too terrible to look on; and thou wilt soon be told. But the Padré Sahib seemed to know him."

"Blessed Mother of God!" exclaimed Maria, sitting down hastily; "it cannot be Diego. What could have brought him here?"

"Diego! Yes, that was the name thy brother called him. But why dost thou ask?"

"He was my malignant enemy, sister."

"And Alla hath delivered thee from him. And thou wilt forgive him, Maria, even as I forgave mine."

"Yes," she replied, slowly, "I will indeed forgive him. See, my brother hath put on his vestment; he is holding up the cross, and the men about are kneeling, and the dying man is confessing his sins. Look!"

It was as she said. And the ghostly confession was proceeding, one of the men holding a cup of cordial to the sufferer's lips as he made motions for it—a broken tale of sin and crime, which we dare not attempt to record. Yet it came forth from the dry, parched lips hardly without a break till its close. Francis d'Almeida had not missed a word; though, from his extreme weakness, Dom Diego had sometimes spoken in low, broken whispers, gasping for breath.

"There is no more to tell," he said, faintly, at its close. "As I shall answer in the judgment, no more. I have hidden nothing; but, with the absolution of the Church, I pray thee let thy sister say, while I can hear and see, 'I forgive thee, Diego,' and I shall then die happy."

Then Francis sent for his sister, and whispered, "It is he. Dost thou forgive him, Maria?"

"Freely and truly," she said, firmly, "as I may be forgiven."

Dom Diego could not speak now, but he could hear the words which fell from the woman he had loved so madly and with so sinful a purpose. He tried to raise his hands, but they fell back on the sheet helples. · and his large bright eyes were glazing fast, and becoming dim. "Maria! Maria! forgive—pardon!" they heard him say in a whisper scarcely audible. And while the Bishop was holding up the cross before him, and preparing to recite the *Beaticum*, she could not resist the impulse, but took the cold hand of the dying man, and said, "I forgive; fear not." Then a soft smile of peace and resignation seemed to pass over his features. "Forgiven," he murmured; and as the words of "Depart, Christian soul, in the name of God the Father Almighty who created thee," were spoken, the spirit passed away with a slight shivering convulsion, and the body lay still in death; and the Bishop and his sister, their sweet voices mingling, chanted the Litany for the dead, which seemed to linger amidst the small domes and grooves of the high roof, echoed, as it were, by angels.

Zóra had stood by spellbound. She had never seen a Christian die; and Maria, who had taught her many hymns, had never chanted to her the Litany for the dead. "Come away," she whispered, when silence fell on all; "come away, and weep in my arms as I have done in thine. Yea, art thou not my sister? and he knew that he was forgiven, and died happy. Surely it was the Lord's doing, and his fate brought him to thy feet. Come away." And Maria, weeping passionately, suffered the girl to lead her to the chamber she had fitted up, and saw her cast herself at the foot of her cross and pray fervently.

Yes, it had been a vast relief to Zóra to go, as her husband and the Queen told her to do, to Maria, and endeavour to keep out the impression which the horrid sights she had seen and the fearful bridge of human carcasses had caused. All day long the girl had never left her Royal mistress's side, and the green dress of the Syud's child had shared the honour of the day with the armour of the Queen and the "standard of the veil." But she hardly in truth knew what she had done; and when, after her prayer, Maria rose calm and at peace, and, taking Zóra to her heart, told her what the wounded who were brought in said of the slight lad who gave cups of water to wounded men, helped them into litters, and still cried his boyish war cry, Zóra hid her blushing face in her sister's breast, and said, "It was not I, Maria; some other, perhaps." But Maria said she need not deny it, for that Abbas Khan would tell her more, and be proud of her to the end of his life. Then Maria bade her return to the Queen; and she departed, saying, "If he will let me come to-morrow, and the Mother does not want me, I will help thee to tend these poor fellows."

Zóra found the Queen where she had left her, but she was more at rest. Her attendants had brought her a small carpet and a pillow, but she had not laid aside her morion and shirt of mail, and she was sitting close to the breach, where the relays of masons were working by the now bright starlight; and the broken wall was rising rapidly course by course. Fortunately the old wall had not been shaken to its foundation, and on clearing away the rubbish the firm portion was soon struck. All through the night the work proceeded steadily; and as day broke about twelve feet in height of the wall had been filled in, and the breach was secure against all chances of sudden attack and surprise. The trenches were not even manned by the enemy; and as day dawned messengers came from the Prince Moorad with a flag of truce, congratulating the Queen on the heroic defence she had made, and informing her that she would hereafter be addressed by the Emperor as Chand Sooltana, the Queen Chand, instead of, as before, the Beebee, or Lady Chand, and begging her permission for the dead to be removed without molestation. And this was granted at once without hesitation. It had, indeed, become necessary to do so, for a sickening stench had already begun to arise from the festering mass, which would have become insupportable had the operation been delayed. But it was a heavy labour. Large gangs of men came by relays; and it was not till the day after, though they worked unremittingly, that the ghastly contents of the ditch were cleared away.

At last, as day was breaking, and a cold fresh wind arose refreshingly from the north, the Queen was persuaded to retire and take rest. What she had gone through, both in body and in mind, during the last two days and nights of the siege and assault, was almost superhuman; but the heroic spirit had never quailed, and she appeared to have no sense of fatigue or want. There was no exultation in her manner, but to Nihung Khan, to Abbas Khan, and the crowd of officers who poured forth their congratulations, she simply said, "I thank the Lord, on whom I depended, and who, by the bravery of ye all, has given us the victory. Be ye as humbly grateful as I am." Zóra helped her to lay aside her armour, bathed her, and clad her in cool garments, and led her to her little King, who was awake, and asking for her. Then as the boy stretched out his arms to her, and she took him, and he stroked her face, with a child's compassionate fondness, the emotion which had been so long pent up in her loving heart burst forth with a violence which terrified those about her. But Zóra laid her down, and soothed her as she would have done an ailing child, till she fell into a deep sleep. There was no tumult of shouting, and cannon, and musketry to arouse her, and peace seemed to have fallen gently upon all.

But for a while only, for the Queen was soon in her accustomed seat in the hall of audience, doing her usual work; and she again wrote to the Beejapoor commanders, informing them of the repulse of the attack, the safety of the fort, and the perilous position of the Moghuls. She urged and entreated her friends to advance at once, when she should be able to make a sally to meet them; and she sent these letters by bold, careful messengers, who, dropping from the fort wall, mingled with the crowds who were removing the dead from the trench, and gained the Moghul lines. Here, however, they were intercepted, and taken to the

Prince, who read the letters, adding what he had done on a former occasion, and inviting the reinforcements to hasten to their destination, as he was most anxious to meet them. "The sooner the better." And they did march at last.

But so slowly. The impetuous Queen, who knew they were near enough to be with them in three days at most, would fain have had them arrive even sooner, and would have helped them to drive the enemy ignominiously from their position. But they scarcely moved at all; certainly not with the desire of crossing swords with their enemies, and it still seemed as if they overrated the power of the Moghul cavalry.

And perhaps they were right, for the cavalry much outnumbered the whole of the Beejapoor forces in advance, and there had been few casualties comparatively out of the thirty thousand horse with which the Prince had left Guzerat. The effect of the nearer approach of the southern forces told, however, seriously on the Moghul camp, which was more straitened than ever for provisions. Prince Moorad would have welcomed heartily any attack by the Beejapoor forces; he could have beaten them easily in the field, and the scope of his action would have been enlarged. He might have gained possession of the upper valley of the Seena, now teeming with plenty—nay, he might have pushed on to Purenda, and established an advanced post there; but it is most probable that the Beejapoor commander had foreseen this, and preferred guarding the approaches to a weak point, rather than obeying the Queen's hasty summons to attack. The Mussulman historians of the period blame the Beejapoor troops heavily for not attacking the Moghuls the day after the assault, or during the assault itself; and their sympathies are entirely with the Queen, who chafed sorely at their delay. But the probability is that their officers were better generals than the Queen, and could see where hidden danger existed clearly enough to avoid it. When she wrote her despatches, however, the morning after the assault, she was in the highest degree sanguine; and when she received her officers at the afternoon durbar there was not a sign of fatigue or care upon her cheerful countenance.

Among others was the Bishop, who, with Maria, had come up to see her before the durbar should commence; and they told her of the death of Dom Diego, in whose gallant advance she had been so deeply interested. Of course the Queen remembered the tale, as she had heard it before her friends went to Goa; but she could hardly be brought to believe that the man who had been mortally wounded in the assault was the same person, until the general outlines of his confession had been related to her. Then, indeed, she took Maria into her arms and congratulated her on her escape. Surely God had specially preserved Maria's honour and her own, and Maria's gratitude had not been lack of expression.

"And now," said the Bishop, "I must acquit myself of my duty to the dead and to the Church and State I serve. I cannot go to Surat myself; but the Prince, who has the reputation of being frank and honourable, may be induced to interest himself for my Government, with whom he is on friendly terms, and receive my explanation of these affairs. I would, therefore, solicit a note to him from your Majesty, and be the bearer of it while the truce lasts."

"It is dangerous, Padré Sahib," returned the Queen, musing. "My own opinion is that he would extort the money, which you say is very considerable, from the banker, and appropriate it to his own use; or that his people, who are notoriously corrupt, would make away with it. But let not this rest on my opinion alone; let us send for Abbas Khan and Nihung Khan, on whose ability and discretion you can depend, and hear what they advise." And they were sent for. Both were hard by, still working at the breach, and they came directly; and the Bishop related to them the facts we already know.

They did not apprehend any personal danger to the Bishop in his proposed visit to the Prince Moorad, but they were decidedly unanimous in advising that he should not be told of Dom Diego's hoard of wealth. The Imperial Government, they said, is, by long established law and usage, heir to all the property of persons who die or are killed in their service, particularly if they are foreigners;

and the issue would be that this treasure would be lost for the purpose for which it is designed. There would be no hope of saving it.

"But suppose," said Nihung Khan, whose opinion, being the elder, carried the most weight, "that you ask the Prince for the horses, arms, and moneys of the deceased now in camp. That will only be a fair demand. If granted, it may open your way to a disclosure of the remainder at another audience. But you will see, Señor Padré," he continued, laughing, "that that will be refused on the grounds I have mentioned. And it is better you should be prepared for the truth, though it may be told in fair words which will give you no offence."

"I dare say you are right, Khan," returned the Bishop. "Dom Diego was buried early, with the rites of the Church, and I am at liberty. There is no time to be lost; and if I go at all, I would beg that the flag of truce be prepared, and that a palanquin be got ready for me."

Maria was very anxious, and now could not restrain her feelings. "Go not, Francis," she cried; "go not among those savage men. Why not wait a few days, and when they are gone thou canst write to the authorities at Goa, and send the letter to King Ibrahim, who will forward it, when the necessary steps can be taken, through the bankers of Goa, to obtain the effects of brother Diego from Surat without giving any power to the Mogul Government to interfere."

"Thou art the wisest counsellor among us, Maria," said the Queen, smiling kindly on her, "and I will send thy brother's despatch to King Ibrahim myself; there will be no doubt he will do what is needful. Bankers are always true, and I see no difficulty whatever. Go, Padré Sahib; my mirdhas shall attend thee with honour, and it may be that the Prince will make political disclosures to thee which may be of importance. Go, prepare thyself, and lose no time, for the day is yet ample for thy purpose."

So the good Bishop set out. No armed men were sent with him, but only four silver mace-bearers, as a sign that he was a Royal ambassador. They were stopped at the first picket near the west end of the trenches, and thence passed on cautiously through the busy camp to Furhut Mahal, where the Prince had taken up his residence, to which a bridge of rough pontoons, or boats, had been thrown across the moat. He had to wait at the head of the bridge till permission was given to advance, and, attended and preceded by the mirdhas, he was ushered into the entrance hall, and thence, following the officer on duty, he ascended the steps which led to the upper storey where, for the sake of its coolness, the Prince had taken up his quarters.

The Prince Moorad, a fair young man of pleasing appearance, but plainly dressed in white muslin, was seated on a pile of cushions, accompanied by three elderly officers, who were evidently of high rank. He partly rose as the Bishop bowed low before him, returned the salute, and bidding him be seated, said, "You speak Persian, sir?"

"Imperfectly," was the reply; "but I am used to speak it to my Queen and in the Court at Beejapoor. I can write it also as I speak it."

"Good," said the Prince; "then tell me why you have come. Are you the ambassador of the Sultana?"

"I have the honour to bear a note from her," and he withdrew it from the sash of his robe, "which will explain the object of my intrusion upon your Highness. Will you be pleased to read it?"

The Prince took the envelope. After having examined the seal, he carefully opened it and read the contents.

"This only states that thou art a Bishop of the Christian Church at Goa; and, as such, thou art welcome. Wilt thou proceed to tell thy business? Is it secret or political?"

"Neither, my Prince," was the reply; "but personal only as regards the effects of one Dom Diego di Fonseca, who was a priest of the Christian Church, and who died of wounds received in the assault yesterday."

"Dead!" cried those present. "Dead! and thou knowest this of a certainty?"

"I dressed his wounds during the night, my lords; but it was hopeless; and I buried him this morning before the sun rose.

"He was a gallant soldier, if a Nazarene priest," said one of the elder officers. "Peace be with his memory, and the peace of God rest upon him."

"Ameen!" murmured the others. "With a hundred like him we had won the fort."

"And thy business, Señor Padré?" asked the Prince.

"The effects of the deceased; his horses, arms, pay. These are for masses, which he willed should be said; and to give peace to his soul, it is necessary they should be performed."

"Yes," said the Prince, smiling; "the Padrés do that at Agra, where the Asylum of the World has built them a church. It is called mass. But what effects had he, Señor Padré?"

"I know not, your Highness; but, he said, though only a humble priest, he had attained rank. He had not speech to tell me what he had, and was too weak to be questioned."

"It is against the law, your Highness," observed one of the secretaries present, "to surrender the effects of one who has died in the State service; but it is competent to you to give any gift in recognition of his death as a gallant soldier, and that will be more acceptable to the good Padré than horses, arms, tents, or elephants, all of which have been appropriated to the Government use."

"I demand nothing," said the Bishop; "but whatever His Highness's generosity may dictate I will take thankfully, be it the smallest sum."

"Nay! the son of Akbar Padshah knows how to be generous,"

said the man who had just spoken. "Permit your slave to send for two hundred mohurs, which will be equal to the value of the Christian's effects;" and, writing a few lines on a slip of paper, the Prince's seal was affixed to it, and calling an attendant it was sent to the treasury.

Most profuse were the Bishop's thanks for, in his estimation, the princely liberality with which he had been treated; and for an instant he thought he had better have brought Dom Diego's document; but the other course, suggested by Maria, was most feasible, and freed him from all responsibility.

"And now," said the Prince, "as thou art a discreet and well-spoken person, and accustomed, no doubt, to the political affairs of Courts, we have a proposition to send, through thee, to the heroic Chand Sooltana, whose fame is spread over Hind, to which we invite her serious consideration." Then he paused for awhile, and resumed—

"Although," he continued, "by the fortune of war we have suffered a repulse from the fort with heavy loss, which has deprived us of many brave comrades and soldiers, yet the might of this army is unimpaired; and I am prepared to resume the siege as soon as the present truce is expired. The Sooltana, we know, is relying upon succour from Beejapoor; but we have read her letters, written only this morning, and forwarded them to their destination. But she will see that it is impossible for the friends she expects to arrive in time to save her. They do not exceed six thousand horse, without artillery; and we have with us thirty thousand of the Imperial cavalry. But we are without cause of war with Beejapoor; and those who watch us we have respected, as they have respected us. If we attack the fort again, which we have determined to do if our proposal is refused, the consequences will be deplorable; for our soldiers, remembering the events of yesterday, will allow none to escape from it, and all must inevitably perish, including the Queen herself and the boy King. The consequences, therefore, rest with her alone; and as a humane and merciful woman she will not provoke them by a false estimate of her own power.

"Listen, therefore, Señor Padré; and you, a man of God and of peace, will not refuse to exert your powers of persuasion with her, too. My generals and myself, that is the Khan Khanan and Khan Jehan Lody—and he introduced them—have this morning, with the aid of my learned secretary, drawn up the draft of a treaty between the kingdom of Ahmednugger and the Imperial Government of Hind, which, if executed, will not only perpetuate the mutual good will of both States, but cement their attachment to each other as long as the Sun and Moon shall endure. This is it," he continued, taking a roll of paper from the secretary's hand; "and I will briefly explain its purport to you.

"We demand no expenses of the war. All the treasures and jewels of Ahmednugger remain in the young King's possession.

"Our Royal army will quit its present position, and retire to its own territories, on guarantee by the Queen of no molestation, and orders for grain and forage to be paid for on delivery.

"In return we demand cession of the province of Berar, which Ahmednugger cannot defend, and which is a scene of disorder and rapine, and a cause of suffering to the country at large. It is not an ancient possession of Ahmednugger, whose proper hereditary dominions are guaranteed, it is a province retaken by treachery from Duria Imad Shah, who asked for aid against an usurping Minister, was imprisoned, and foully murdered. No one can deny this, Señor Padré, for it is as notorious as the Sun at noonday, and has long cried for justice at the hands of the Asylum of the World, my father.

"And now, Señor Padré, you have permission to depart. Take these in memory of the son of Akbar Padshah, who presents them to you;" and, taking a small rosary of pearls from his neck, he hung them round that of the Bishop, while a mirdha in attendance threw a light Cashmere shawl over his shoulders. "And my good wishes for your success with the Sultana, to whom I forward by you my sincere admiration and respects. The sum on account of the Christian cavalier you will find in your palanquin."

Then the Bishop rose, and took leave. "I will do my best to stay further carnage, O Prince," he said, "but the question must rest with Her Majesty the Queen and her advisers." Then he was conducted to his palanquin, and passed out of the camp as he had come.

## CHAPTER VI.

### PEACE FOR AWHILE.

IT was yet day when Francis d'Almeida again reached the fort; and, after giving an account to Maria of the result of his embassy, and the liberal conduct of the Prince Moorad, he looked round his patients, and sent word to the Queen that he had been entrusted by the Prince with a political message which he could deliver to no one but herself; and, if she were at leisure, he would come to her presence directly, and would prefer seeing her alone at first. The result of the Bishop's mission had been what the Queen expected, and she did not hesitate to request his attendance as quickly as possible.

"I have only Zóra with me," said the Queen, when the Bishop was ushered into her presence. "There has been much to dictate, and I always feel more confidence with her, and more at my ease than with the men. But what news hast thou brought, Señor Padré? and how didst thou succeed in regard to the effects of the cavalier?"

"They would not give them to me," he replied, "as I was told they would not; but the Prince gave me a heavy purse of gold instead, which is amply sufficient—nay, a munificent gift; but methinks," continued the good man, simply, "if I had told him of the rest, it would have been confiscated. I had better obtain it through the banker with whom it is in deposit. But that is a minor matter altogether; I have much more important news to communicate to your Majesty, which relates to peace."

"Ha!" cried the Queen, clapping her hands; "so they are tired of war after the game they have played, and its consequences."

"No; your Majesty must not be deceived nor deceive yourself," returned the Bishop. "They are determined to renew the war, to reopen the siege, and to continue it until the fort is taken, and every one in it put to the sword. This is what the soldiers demand, and cry out for almost to mutiny."

"Yes," said the Queen, sadly; "we might perish, all of us, but never yield; there the Prince is right. But what terms of peace does the Prince offer?"

"He gave me this memorandum, which hath his own seal," was the reply. "Perhaps you had better read it yourself."

"Let Zóra read it, Señor. I have not patience to think of it. Remember how unprovoked this war was, and how I strove to avert it. But read, Zóra, and let us hear the worst."

Except for an expression of impatience now and again with her hands, the Royal lady heard the document to the end. "Some of it is fair, and some unfair," she said at length. "It is true we have no hope of aid from Beejapoor. When its troops might have struck in and made the Prince's position untenable, they kept aloof, and abandoned me to my fate. Oh, that Abbas Khan had led them! or why not the King himself? Has he forgotten the many times this poor life has been imperilled for him and his? But now," she continued, bitterly, "a new building, a new ornament to his palace, a new falcon or hunting leopard, has more attraction for him than his mother who made him what he is. Let it pass, it is my fate; and we have—thanks be to Thee, just and merciful Alla!—been able to defend ourselves hitherto, and may defy the worst, even death."

"If it were thine own only, noble Queen," said the Bishop, respectfully, "it might be welcome to thee amid all the factions, intrigues, and perils thou hast to endure; but, remember, thou art accountable to God for the lives of all who are entrusted to thee as His viceregent, and there are thousands here who look to thee."

"Death!" she cried, excitedly; "did I not court it in the assault? Can anyone say that I blenched from it, or hid myself in my zenana?"

"No one, lady," returned the Bishop. "On the contrary, thine enemies do thee ample justice, and were even full of praise of thy heroism; and they would not have it subjected to the last trial in death. Consider, honoured lady, how many lives may be saved if terms can be made. But forgive me if I have spoken too freely on this matter."

"Nay, but only as a peaceful minister of the Lord," she returned, gracefully. "As to the cession of Berar, I for one would not oppose it. Its annexation was the act of a madman. He who murdered his own father cruelly, to whom massacre was familiar, and who destroyed the Royal family of Berar, was hardly accountable for his actions upon earth; and I for one would cheerfully resign all pretension to Berar, which from the first hath carried the consequences of its sin-laden possession with it. The country never belonged to this kingdom, and its retention only embroils us with other parties, and it also lies too distant to be defended as it needs with these troubles to meet at home."

"And were Berar ceded, your Majesty will observe that the King Bahadur will be guaranteed his throne, and there will be no interference with any part of his ancient dominions—which is worthy of especial consideration."

"It would be if I could trust those that make it; but my soul tells me that the lion has only tasted blood, and would have more. Nevertheless, I will lay all before my council in durbar this evening, and will not delay an answer."

The evening durbar was numerously attended; all the principal officers and Ministers were present, and brought forward their recommendations for rewards to those who had distinguished themselves by acts of valour; and these having been granted, the general assembly was dissolved, and those only remained whom the Queen specified.

"First, my lords," said the Queen, "I desire to know from you all, unreservedly, in what condition you find the fort to be after the siege, up to the present time. My reasons for the question are urgent, and I will state them presently."

Then every department was reviewed. Except at the breach where the mine had been sprung, the fortifications were uninjured, as there had been no attack on three sides; but the mine, though but little of the wall had fallen, had shaken it for a considerable distance on each side, cracks were opening in it in various places, and it would require to be taken down and built from the foundation ere it could bear any fresh cannonade, even from smaller guns than had been employed; "and," added the engineer (for so we may call him), "any chance shot might strike a weak part and bring down masses of the masonry, which would render the fort defenceless on the side that has been attacked. I and the chief builders have examined the whole, and that is our decided opinion."

Many others followed. The powder and shot were much expended, and most of the new powder had been used. The old was not sound, and must be renewed, and shot was needed, but all the guns were in good condition.

The already long-continued siege had caused the expenditure of much provisions. About two weeks' supply remained, which might be extended for some days more, but there was no possibility of receiving any from without, as the enemy guarded the approaches to the fort so closely, and had already intercepted several large convoys of grain and ghee.

In fine, the general result of the report was unsatisfactory. If half the garrison could be dispensed with, provisions might hold out; but the condition of the wall was a peril which could not be remedied, and in regard to it there was not one dissentient voice. Then the Queen produced the draft she had received from Prince Moorad. "If," she said, "our condition for defence had been what I hoped it would be, I would have destroyed this paper, and allowed affairs to go on as they have begun; but as it is, ye, my lords, should know of it, and bear me witness that I have concealed nothing from you. Had my unworthy people of Beejapoor behaved as I expected they would, we should not have been reduced to these straits; but as they are, they are of no use to us, and the few that watch the Manikdown Hills are too weak to advance against thirty thousand Moghuls."

"It is true," said Nihung Khan, with a sigh; "they are too weak to effect more than they are doing now, straitening the supplies of the Moghul army. Yet that cannot be depended upon, since the King of Khandesh, it is well known, is now sending up large convoys from his dominions by the northern passes, which we cannot prevent, and with them come some heavy guns. All these will arrive in the course of a few days at furthest, and the Prince does not exaggerate his resources to prolong the siege. And how could we repair the wall to meet it?"

"They are clever men, these Moghul engineers," said the engineer officer who had before spoken. "We found, this morning, as we examined the counterscarp, that five other places had been mined to be blown in. There was not time apparently to complete or load the mines, else we should have been attacked in several points at once. They depended upon the effect of the five mines, which, but for the humane man who proclaimed them, would have been fired at once, and the side of the fort blown completely open; and they can do the same again."

These ominous words fell with terrible effect on the ears of all that heard them. The question was no longer one of opinion, it was one of necessity. Was the fort tenable at all?

"Let your servant," said Abbas Khan, "go to Soheil Khan, who commands the forces at Shahdroog. If he could be persuaded to march to our aid, all these proud Moghuls might be chased from the field."

"But that would involve a delay of nearly a month, even if he marched at once," said the Queen.

"And in the condition of the wall, I could not guarantee it to stand under fire for two days," said the engineer. "I have no thought of life, as I say this; but I think on the helpless women and children, and the men who must perish before a ruthless assault which the Prince suggests, and which we, were we in the place of the Moghuls, should make. Remember that though the fort is hard of access, yet it is impossible of egress. No one can escape from it."

The Queen then laid before all assembled the question of Berar. For her own part, she desired not to retain it. Ever since the kingdom had possessed it, misfortune and war had come with it, as was known to all. It need never have been taken; and cruel murder had been necessary to its retention.

Thus the subject was debated for some hours with animation. The Bishop was called and asked whether he had been directed to carry any message to the Prince Moorad from the Queen; but his account of the object of his mission and its results, and his assurance that the draft of the treaty must have been prepared beforehand, as the Prince's seal was only affixed in his presence, assured all that the proposal was spontaneous; and after a further brief consultation, it was accepted, with some slight modification, and despatched by the hands of Abbas Khan and Nihung Khan the next day. And no further objections being made, the treaties were mutually exchanged the day following, when a great portion of the Moghul army had already marched.

What a relief their departure was to all! How quiet the fort was now! No discharge of cannon night and day; no danger from missiles; no distress for water, which had before become serious, and for which there was no remedy. The people of the city, who for the most part had all retired to the villages at some distance, flocked back, opened their shops and secret stores of grain, and all was once more as it had been; while the public rejoicings at the victory of the assault and the departure of their bitter enemies were splendid, and attended by munificent distributions of charity in every portion of the kingdom.

The Queen's first care was for the wall, which was found, as the engineer officer of the fort had declared, in a perilous condition, and was taken down with difficulty, and not without risk to life. It was rebuilt, wherever necessary, from the very foundation. All the mined galleries of the Moghuls were traced, and inspected by the Queen in person, who could the more perfectly understand, with gratitude for the escape, the danger that the fort and all within it had escaped. In the guarantee of the dominions of the kingdom, too, she felt an increased assurance for the future; and could she only avert the misery arising from domestic faction, a terror always present, she might expect a peaceful minority, and the respect and sympathy of all surrounding kingdoms. Of the Moghuls she had no dread then. The man who had originally written to the Prince Moorad to invite his interference was detained at Beejapoor, and evinced no disposition for fresh intrigue. She therefore caused the young King Bahadur to be crowned again, and his further residence at the fort of Chawund was no longer necessary, the Queen herself taking charge of him.

It was wonderful to see, too, how rapidly and surely the internal administration was reformed—in fact, re-created. The revenue survey and assessments that Mullek Umber's great genius had suggested were carried on as fast as possible, to the satisfaction of the people, and the revenues were collected without unequal pressure, and were ample for all expenses of the State, affording, indeed, a large surplus. Outwardly, therefore, and to all appearance, the kingdom was at peace.

Nor was there any change in the circumstances of the persons whose affairs have supplied the events of this tale. The Bishop and his sister, as the country became quiet, were able to make excursions to Aurungabad, always a source of gratification. And once the Bishop, taking advantage of the return of some cavalry to Beejapoor, visited his flock there, and was satisfied at its progress. He found the Queen Taj-ool-Nissa the mother of a fine boy; and as she put it into his arms, she besought his blessing on the child, which he gave solemnly. All his old friends welcomed him; and even the bitter priest had many a kind word for the man who, as all believed, had fought valiantly on the side of the truth of Islam in the battle of the "Standard of the Veil," for so the defence of the fort against the Moghuls had become known among the people of the country.

With the King he had many earnest private conversations in regard to the future, which to his view was full of apprehension and danger. "It was not that I would not, but that I dare not provoke a war with Prince Moorad which would set the whole of the Dekhan in a flame. One by one the kingdoms of the north—Guzerat, Malwa, and Khandesh—have fallen. The Queen-Mother does not see her danger; but the Nizam Shahis and all that belonged to them have ever been treacherous, and she may yet rue the hour in which she trusted them. But I know—we all know—her heroism and self-devotion, and she will die at her post rather than abandon it. And yet, Padré Sahib, if she could be persuaded to leave Ahmednugger and come to us she would be received with all our old affection and loyalty."

"I will do what I can," was the invariable reply to many such conversations; "but your Majesty knows her inflexible and honourable nature, and nothing less than being driven from her position would induce her to abandon it." I think, however, that had it not been for what had transpired in regard to his sister, that the Bishop would have been well content to have settled finally at Beejapoor, visiting Moodgul and a new mission at Cheetapoor, among the distillers and saga makers, which his zealous coadjutor had organised; but there was no mention of his sister, nor any invitation from the Queen Taj-ool-Nissa, and it was evident that for some time to come Beejapoor was no place for her.

Of Osman Beg the Bishop could hear nothing. His father had returned from Mecca, and, at first, resided on a small property which he had retained; but he had died, and his possessions had lapsed to the State. Osman Beg had, it was supposed, joined the Moghul army, but where he was serving in its wide empire no one seemed to know or care.

There was no change whatever in the situation of Abbas Khan and Zóra. He continued to hold the command of the fort and the troops within it, and so long as the Queen lived, or remained there, he determined to abide with her. He was not ambitious of employment in civil or political affairs, and he had an instinctive dislike and mistrust of all the hereditary offices of the Ahmednugger State; of those constant petty and vexatious intrigues against each other which seemed to him, though peace from without appeared more and more confirmed, to be dangerous in their machinations, and which must, ere long, burst into open contention. Except this, nothing occurred to disturb the serenity of their lives. Their little excursions to villages round about, such as Bhatoree and others, to the Royal gardens, and to the pretty little country palace, which is known now by the name of "The Happy Valley," all served to pass the time pleasantly; and the Queen

Regent had ever work for Zóra to do in the drafts of private correspondence which she carried on. Zóra, too, was now the mother of a fine boy, and the pride of her husband and herself in the thriving, crowing, little fellow cannot, I think, be exaggerated. They were lovers in the truest sense of the word, cheering and supporting each other: she, a companion to him, whose bravery and work had been amply tried; he, to her, the same as she had watched over first in the fearful night at Juldroog, which had had so deep an influence over their lives. But the political events of the time were more and more threatening, and were not to be averted either by former treaty or by the wisdom or heroic perseverance of the Queen; and the details of the local historian, Ferishta, form a melancholy record of the last struggles of the unhappy and distracted kingdom. Without entering too much into historical details they may be briefly sketched, so as to render Queen Chand's position intelligible.

Retaining Nihung Khan as commander of the forces, as he lacked administrative ability, she had appointed Mahomed Khan, an hereditary officer of much experience, to the general direction of affairs, and for a time all went prosperously. But the ambition of Mahomed Khan was not proof against the temptation to increase his power, and he confined Nihung Khan, aspiring himself to become Regent, and to deprive the Queen of all authority whatever. This the Royal lady resisted, and wrote urgently to her nephew, King Ibrahim, to send her such a force as would keep the rebellious Minister in check. To no one better than Abbas Khan, whose friendship for Nihung Khan was sincere, could she entrust this delicate negotiation. The King would hear from him the true state and danger of affairs at Ahmednugger; nor would he, she knew, be slow to urge, or lack eloquence in urging, the necessity of interposing to prevent further pretext for intervention by the Moghuls, which was the point most especially to be dreaded. We need not describe particulars of this journey to Beejapoor, nor of the political discussions there; nor yet of Abbas Khan's happy meeting with his uncle and aunt, and many old friends; but he was successful in the object of his mission. Soheil Khan was despatched with a sufficient force, which arrived at Ahmednugger in safety; but the Beejapoor troops found that their entry was opposed by the usurper, but the garrison, being faithful, seized him and made him over to the Queen. Meanwhile, however, Mahomed Khan had despatched letters to Khan Khanan, the Moghul general then in Berar, praying for assistance, as he was holding the country in trust for the Emperor of Dehli. Had this been discovered at the time, it is hardly possible that the usurper would have escaped with his life; but he was spared, Nihung Khan was released and appointed to the chief authority, and the Queen's power being reestablished, the troops from Beejapoor were dismissed with handsome presents and grateful thanks.

The Moghuls, however, as Soheil Khan learned on his way back, had occupied districts much to the south of Berar, and he wrote to the King of Beejapoor for instructions. The King ordered him to stand fast on the Godavery river, and sent a large reinforcement aided by troops from Golconda. These allied troops advanced against the Moghuls; but after a bloody general engagement, which lasted for two days, victory remained with the Moghuls. Now the Queen Chand had sent to the assistance of the Beejapoor troops a number of her own for defence against aggression, and it is possible this was considered a cause for the new war which had commenced so inauspiciously.

Strange as it may appear, Nihung Khan, regardless of danger from without, now endeavoured to destroy the power of his benefactress. Indeed, he had attained so much local power that, inflated by pride, he sent a force to invest the town of Beer, which is situated to the south of the river Godavery, and to which the aggressions of the Moghuls had extended. He also made an attempt to invade Berar, but both these movements being unsupported, failed of effect, and he returned to Ahmednugger.

These continued disturbances naturally attracted the attention of the Emperor Akbar. His son, the Prince Moorad, had died during their continuance, not long, indeed, after the victory over the combined forces of Beejapoor; and the Emperor, now determined to prosecute the war in person, marched to the south, captured the important fortress of Asseergurh, and directed his second son, Prince Daniel Mirza, with Khan Khanan, his chief general, to undertake operations against the fort and kingdom of Ahmednugger.

## CHAPTER VII.

### THE SECOND SIEGE OPENS.

THE political events sketched in the last chapter occupied upwards of two years, and bring down the action of this tale and the Queen's life to the close of 1598, or commencement of 1599. Nihung Khan, foiled in his ill-considered attack on Berar, in which he had been entirely unsupported by the allies of Ahmednugger, and out-manœuvred besides by the General Khan Khanan, burned all his heavy baggage on the borders of Berar, at the head of the pass he was unable to descend, and fled back to Ahmednugger. Here he vainly tried to make terms with the Queen and regain his old place. But she refused to admit one to her councils who, though a man of high renown, was fatally rash and untrustworthy; and having no other place of refuge, he fled the country and was seen no more. After their bloody defeat in the Godavery, the Beejapoor and Golconda troops made no further attempt to check the advancing enemy; and that defeat had, there is no doubt, already decided the fate of the Ahmednugger kingdom; and as the monsoon of 1598 broke up, the Emperor Akbar ordered the forces under his son Daniel and Khan Khanan to advance without delay. With Queen Chand no commander of note remained in the field. All the troops on which she could have relied to check the enemy's advance were broken and much separated, and to bring them together would be a work of labour for which there was no time, and neither Beejapoor nor Golconda were in the humour to risk further collisions with the Imperial army by an advance. What troops it was possible to collect and organise, Abbas Khan, ever steady and faithful, collected about the city, and the fort was put in as complete order as possible, and provisioned liberally for six months.

To the command of the garrison Humeed Khan was appointed, originally a Beejapoor eunuch attached to the Queen's palace for many years. She had brought him with her on the last occasion ; and, as he had been well educated and displayed soldier-like qualities, he had been employed in the field, and had on all occasions distinguished himself by valour and sagacity. In the first siege of the fort he had been selected both by Nihung Khan and Abbas Khan for command of a large portion of the garrison ; and his valour on the repulse of the attack and in the general defence was as valuable as it was remarkable. Nor with these antecedents was it at all strange that he should be selected for the post he now held, with the approval of all, for he was popular with the soldiery ; and had succeeded in uniting all in a determination to stand by the young King to the last, and defend their fortress to the utmost.

But it was seen and observed by all that a tone and manner of despondency possessed the Queen which was new to her character. Her only solace seemed to be the boy Bahadur, who, now about five years old, returned her affection with tenderness and a child's loving consideration; and as she often strained him passionately to her breast, would cry, "Weep not, O grandmother; when I am a man I will make all bad men thy slaves; and we will be so happy, and no tears shall come again." Yes, the little fellow seemed to be a great solace and comfort to her. Not that she put Zóra aside, or Maria, for they were her daily companions as before; but she made no new friends, and the old ones she felt had their own vocations and cares in life, which occupied and interested them more than those of, as she said, a worn-out old woman.

Yet it was not so. Never at any period of their lives had Maria or Zóra loved her more devotedly or fondly; and the patience and submission with which she endured all her vexatious troubles, and the heroism and cheerful trust with which she now prepared to meet new perils, gave her additional interest in their eyes. To all others she preserved her old calm demeanour. She held her durbars as usual. Every point of the administration was reviewed and checked as of old; Zóra had her appointed private tasks allotted to her, and, with Abbas Khan and his officers, every question regarding the completeness for defence and organisation of the defenders was discussed with her usual wisdom. But in the quiet hours, when business did not occupy her, it was plainly visible that anxiety very often cast her down, almost beyond the power of raising herself again. At such times, if they asked her why she wept, she could not tell them, except that it seemed to her she was being drawn away from earth and all she most loved, and so the Lord was preparing her for Paradise; and as the present was her true Paradise, it grieved her to change it, and so she wept. Before her was a mystery; here there was no mystery, only the homage of loving hearts. They are wrong, she used to tell them, who prayed for death as a release from trouble and suffering. Rather let all live on that life may be purified, and the spirit exalted, till God sees fit to take it, as He will when He has purified and chastened it. And thus, she said to all, she was being prepared, and they were to rejoice when she wept rather than sorrow.

How thoughtful was she for them all! She was evidently most anxious for Maria. "Thou art more tender of heart," she would say, "than we tough Moslems. Thy faith is more tender; and the scenes thou hast endured with us here are not fit either for thee or thy brother, and ye must leave me till the peril be past. If it pass, and we have peaceful lives before us till my boy grows up, thou and thy brother shall roam where ye will, and preach as ye will; for who does not love and honour ye?"

It was a bitter parting; but the Queen sent Maria and her

brother away. A body of men came from Dowlutabad, sent by Mullek Umber to escort treasure for the pay of the troops with the Queen; and the Queen sent the Bishop and his sister with them to her faithful friend. It was the only opportunity there might be for many weeks; and if peace ensued, they could at any time return again in a few days. And Maria had been absent before, and had returned safely; so Zóra was comforted, but not the Queen.

The evening before the small force marched, Maria and the Queen were alone together, and the Royal lady, taking Maria's head on her breast, said gently, "Thou hast been a true and loving daughter to me, child. All the women of my country are feeble and impetuous; but from the first even unto the last thou hast been the same. Thou hast borne with a weak old woman's waywardness; thou hast put sweet loving thoughts into my heart, and told me truths which well up, and teach me mercy. And oh, Maria! though I have never mentioned it to thee, how can I thank thee for thy conduct at Beejapoor; so gentle, yet so firm. Thou dost not know, thou never canst know, how he pleaded with me for thee, or what he offered me for thee. And he, too, is loving, and would have been kind and faithful to thee; and at first I grieved that it could not be. But thou wast right. The Lord vouchsafed wisdom to thee, and thou art blessed with that thought, O, my daughter; for when ye meet, all will have passed away in peace.

He is the father of children now, and is happy; though he hath not forgotten her who was a joy to him. I would often fain have spoken to thee about that eventful passage in thy young life; but these are my last words to thee, and thou wilt not forget them."

"Never, never! my more than mother," she returned, sobbing bitterly. "And may the Lord grant that we meet again in peace." She would have said more, for her heart was full of gratitude; but the Queen said gently,—

"It may not be, daughter. My message is coming nearer to me; nearer, nearer, day by day, and I am content. Go now, and leave me, with but one embrace—the last. I shall think of thee in safety, till the angel summons me. Lo!" and she stretched her hand on high, while a smile of triumph spread over her features, and her still lustrous eye glowed brightly, "Lo! he is near me, even now."

* * * *

We have already said there was no force in the field which could pretend to check the advance of the powerful army which was now approaching by safe and easy stages. The siege train was especially powerful and its equipment complete, and the Emperor had sent a large body of the famous miners of the northern provinces, who in their peculiar vocation were unsurpassed in skill and daring. Khan Khanan, who knew the ground perfectly, had determined to risk as few of his own troops' lives as possible, and he had already seen proved how comparatively easy and how certain it would be to destroy the fort with gunpowder.

Osman Beg was in his place as general leader and director of the marches, and he had gained the confidence of the commander-in-chief with singular adroitness and plausibility. All these intervening years the mad craving of his heart for Zóra had never diminished, nay, it had fed on its own imaginings. What would she not be now in the full possession of her matured beauty? How different to the poor Fakeer's daughter of Juldroog, whom he had so madly loved. No one, he believed, knew that he belonged to the Moghul forces at all. His name was a common one among the bodies of Turcomans who served in the Imperial army, and in the first siege he had kept himself aloof from the camp and the siege operations. Dom Diego had asked him to command a portion of the storming party, and even taunted him with cowardice when he refused; but Osman Beg had laughed at the possibility of taking the fort as the priest imagined, and he heard of his death without surprise and without regret. "Mine shall be a sure game," he thought; "one in which the risk will be small and the reward certain. Then I shall gloat myself with revenge, and my virtuous cousin shall die at my feet or be hurled into the air to feed the vultures. Let but our position become securely taken up before the fort, and I will see what Moghul gold may not effect within.

The last march was made. The people of the city and its environs, warned by previous experience, had deserted their homes for some days, and nothing was left in the streets but starving, homeless dogs, who howled piteously night and day. There was nothing on the plain but the grim old fort and its defences, which the Moghul commander could see were in much more complete order than they had previously been. The wide esplanade was cleared of every vestige of cover; trees all around had been cut down; the defences of the parapets had been newly topped with clay; loopholes had been narrowed, and embrasures protected by sandbags and gabions. Even the covered way at the crest of the counterscarp had been cleared out and fitted for musketeers, and larger guns than before mounted in many places on the broad rampart and the bastions. The work had been that of months, and Abbas Khan was not one who would trust to others to see it performed. He and the Queen had passed their days on the ramparts, and during working hours the red umbrella of the Queen could be seen by the whole garrison, moving from point to point; while at night she went the accustomed rounds in her turn, with other officers, generally accompanied by Humeed Khan. So far as human means and the science of the time could ensure security, Ahmednugger was safe.

And the Moghul commander felt that it was so, and that all the skill of his own engineers would be needed to meet the preparations. After the first reconnaissance, in which he lost many men from the combined fire of the fort and the garrison of the covered way, the trenches were carried on by sap as before. But the defenders of the covered way, led by brave and enterprising officers, attacked the trenches at night, cut off the workmen, and vexed the whole operation until it made very slow progress in comparison with what it had done on the first occasion. These skirmishes, too, cost the defenders little in comparison with the terror they inflicted. The hardy Mahratta Mawalees, from the western ghauts, who afterwards became so famous under Sivagee, fell on the enemy with their national shouts of "Hur! Hur! Mahadeo!" sword in hand, and seemed insensible to danger. Showers of arrows were shot into the trenches, and if pursued by the Moghuls, the lightly equipped Mahrattas ran back into their galleries, and crossed into the ditch and fort by the sally-ports which had been opened. As yet no attempt had been made upon the defences of the fort, and the garrison grew more confident even than before. The siege did not progress, and the young Prince Daniel and Khan Khanan grew impatient, for they well knew if there were the least sign of failure the Beejapoor and Golconda armies would be again in motion.

One of the chief leaders of these daring night attacks was a young Mahratta chief, one of the Sirkay family, who, with his cousin Peelagee, were hereditary officers of the Nizam Shahy kingdom, and had brought their own retainers to the defence of the fort. Both were famed for personal valour of no ordinary kind, and the Sirkay Mawalees had established a reputation for boldness in their peculiar manner of attack, which had gained them deserved fame. Their post was in the covered way in the south-east angle of the ditch, which enabled them to make flank attacks which were most annoying to the enemy; and this being part of the particular command of Humeed Khan, he had several times brought them to the Queen's notice, and had them rewarded by rings and anklets of gold, and other valuable gifts. As if to vex Abbas Khan, with whom he had had some slight difference, he said to Sirkay one evening, "Let me come with ye to-night, and witness what ye let Abbas Khan share in, but not me." So it was arranged, and taking as few of his followers as possible, Humeed Khan went to the post at night, and, led by Sirkay, the Mawalees were soon on the crest of the glacis, crouching like wild animals, to watch their opportunity. That night, however, the breaches seemed deserted. The men had been withdrawn, probably expecting an attack; and Sirkay would have returned, but Humeed said, laughing, "As we are here, we may as well see for ourselves what is doing, and whether the general is mining, as I shrewdly suspect he is."

So they proceeded warily and cautiously, leaving the men behind; but, on turning the angle of a trench, a party of men burst upon them and secured them. Both gave themselves up for lost, for under such circumstances life was little worth; but, instead of putting them to death, they were taken roughly to an officer who sat near a covered way, which some men by the light of torches were driving on. It had been Osman Beg's turn of duty that night in the trenches, and he had taken up as secure a position as possible; and he recognised Humeed Khan in an instant, who at once saluted him wonderingly.

"Dost thou know that I could behead thee at once as a spy?" said Osman Beg.

"I know it," returned the other; "and there would be one man in Ahmednugger the less, that is all. Nor would Abbas Khan, perhaps, be sorry to lose me."

"Then ye are enemies?"

"Not so, openly; but he hates me. He it is who hath vexed ye with sallies; and as I would not be sent on one by him, I have come myself to-night."

"And the Queen?"

"She is much what you remember her, but, methinks, weary of the war. She would like to get safe to Joonair, and give up the place. She does not say this openly, but that is in her heart."

"We shall take it from her, brother."

"Never," replied Humeed Khan. "She will perish in the ruins, but she will never yield."

"And Abbas Khan?"

"You know what he is, Meeah, only prouder and haughtier than he was; and he will never leave the Queen."

"And his wife, Zóra? Dost thou see her?"

"I see her, Meeah! She is more beautiful than ever she was; and he dotes on her like a fool."

"I owe him revenge for what happened at Juldroog, and for what happened in the Palace."

"And thou sayest she is thy wife. What wouldst thou give me for her?"

"I have little to give; but hark! ere we part. Give me the fort by any means thou wilt, and we may both be rich and free. Canst thou come again?"

"Not as I have done to-night; but I may be able to send a message. Now let me escape, and pretend to pursue me;" and Humeed Khan dashed on at his utmost speed, striking down one of the men who had held Sirkay apart. Sirkay shook himself free of the other, narrowly escaping a sword cut, and they soon rejoined the men they had left behind, who fired a volley of arrows to check the pursuers, and made their way into the fort.

"That was a narrow chance, my friend," said Humeed Khan, when he had regained his breath; "but the fellow was too busy asking me questions to see that his men held me fast. But they seemed half asleep, and I watched my opportunity to shake myself free."

"I had given up hope, my lord," was Sirkay's reply; "and I havc to thank you for your part in my escape. We must be more cautious in future."

## CHAPTER VIII.

### THE LAST TRAGEDY.

THE eunuch reflected deeply on the strange adventures of the night. He had known Osman Beg from boyhood, when he was the companion of Abbas Khan. He knew the story of Abbas Khan's love for Zóra, and was present at Osman Beg's trial before the durbar at Beejapoor, when Osman Beg was banished, and it was strange that he should meet him again under such circumstances. But he was not surprised that his hate for his cousin continued in all its bitter virulence. The eunuch had been jealous of Abbas Khan from the first, and he was now compelled to bear his authority and submit to his directions; and such jealousy soon turns to hate. He might make his own terms, perhaps, through Osman Beg, with the Moghul general about the fort. Its possession would be an immense assistance to the Emperor's plans, and its betrayal would be richly rewarded. As to the Queen, he hated her because she had placed him in a subordinate position under her minion; and what would it signify what became of her? She was out of place now. There would be no great difficulty in communicating with Osman Beg, and he trusted to his good luck to carry on the intercourse that had been so strangely begun.

At his morning audience of the Queen the eunuch detailed the events of the night, which were entirely corroborated by Sirkay. Both the Queen and Abbas Khan, while they rebuked them for rashness, none the less praised them for their act of valour; and the eunuch gave his opinion that what he had seen was either the head of a new mine, or a shaft into one which had been begun at a greater distance; and this was what Abbas Khan dreaded. This was no noisy siege. On the contrary, the silence was often oppressive; and the hum of thousands which filled the enemy's camp, the boom of kettledrums, and the music which played before the Royal pavilion, were for the most part the only sounds heard from without; while from within there was nothing to fire at, and the large stone shots from the mortars, which were dropped at random in the direction of the enemy's camp, were frequently the only shots fired by the gunners of the fort. It appeared to the soldiers of the garrison as if the enemy were afraid to attack the fort as they had done on the first occasion, and their vaunting and self-confidence were unbounded. Whenever the Queen went abroad on her usual rounds on the walls, she was met with assertions that the enemy were afraid; that the Moghuls would some day abandon their fortress and march back as they came. But, though she did not undeceive them, she became more and more anxious; and, on his part, Abbas Khan well remembered what Khan Khanan had impressed upon him at his interview with the Prince Moorad regarding the first treaty, that if the siege were renewed, it would be by mines under the fort itself, which would be destroyed with all it held; and that this operation was now in progress there could be little doubt.

Alas! there was now no friendly voice to give them warning, as before, of existing danger, and implore them not to make a useless sacrifice of their lives. The proceedings were of the stern character of the eminent soldier who directed them, who never knew sympathy for an enemy who defied him.

How often Abbas Khan besought the Queen, even with tears, to save herself and the King. It might be done; he felt assured that no enterprise would be more welcome to the Mahratta Mawallees than to carry her with them in a night sortie, and to conduct them by bye-paths, and after their own fashion, to Joonair. Then it mattered little what became of the fort. Those who remained could make terms, and, in the western fastnesses, the King would be safe against all attacks from without, and could rest securely till happier times. "As to all you would leave behind, we should be in the hands of the Lord," he pleaded; "for as soon as you and the boy were gone, we might hold out for a time as a point of honour, and make terms by which every life would be saved. As to the treasure, let it perish, mother, if I could not, as I might, offer a ransom for the fort. I say, let it perish. Is there not enough for all in Chawund and Joonair to suffice for many years?"

Thus, day by day, he pleaded, but still she would not listen. It seemed to her a dishonourable act to desert those who had stood by her with such valour and devotion all through her trials. What care or wish had she for life, except with honour? What would be said of her, but that the Queen who had fought the fearful "Battle of the Veil" had absconded secretly from her people at night to save her own life, leaving all to perish! No! if death were nigh, let it come to her there; she should be blessed.

But there was restlessness in her mind which she could not overcome. Zóra felt she had no longer power over her. She, too, had implored her Royal mistress to save herself and the boy she now loved; and the boy's mother, feeling that with the Queen he would be safe, had besought Queen Chand not to think of her, whom no one would molest by herself, and to carry him away to Joonair, which, against all attacks from without, was impregnable. But, as we have said, the Queen's mind was restless. She felt unable to decide on any course, and many arguments on both sides impelled her first in one direction then in another, which were alike impossible to her on further thought; and she had only to go out among the garrison to hear the old war cries of Beejapoor, and her own country, to feel that she was yet a Queen, and, before God, responsible for all, and no steps were taken either for flight with the Mawallees, or to obtain terms from the Moghuls.

During this period Osman Beg had not been idle. He had contrived to see the eunuch many times at night; and, after the first chance interview with him, he had gone boldly to Khan Khanan, and had privately communicated to him that he had an old Beejapoor friend in the fort, who was, in fact, its commander, and that, if he were authorised, he could enter into negotiations with him for its betrayal, or its capture by surprise. Khan Khanan felt no scruple as to the means of attaining possession of a place which had already cost him so dear, and the capture of which by siege would probably extend so long; and the miners were already complaining of the hardness of the ground in the mines on which they most relied, which were to be sprung inside the walls, and not without much risk and difficulty. Humeed Khan was brought to him once, at night. Khan Khanan was then assured of the perfect condition of the fort, the high spirits of the garrison, and the inflexible determination of Abbas Khan to defend the place to the last extremity. "He is searching for mines daily," said the eunuch, "and should one be discovered, your whole work would be checked indefinitely."

"The difficulty, then, lies with the Queen and Abbas Khan," said the general.

"It does," replied the eunuch; "but it is not insurmountable; and I know for certain that if they are offered honourable terms of capitulation, and permission to remove all property from the fort, except guns and arms, they would agree to them."

"That would be impossible," said the general; "we have the game in our own hands, and we are ready to play it out. What is a month, or even more, to us? To them it is life or death. Were they to propose terms, indeed, it would be very different; but I know nothing less than unconditional surrender would satisfy the Emperor, and I am not prepared to modify that. I suppose," he added with a sneer, "your valiant Dekhanies would not give up their arms."

"They would not," said the eunuch; "and no one dare propose that to them."

"Not even the Queen?"

"Not even she. Her life would be the instant forfeit."

"Now," continued the general, grimly, "suppose that such a report were spread as would raise a tumult among your Dekhanies. We might take advantage of it."

"You might, my lord.

"And we should be successful?"

"That I cannot answer for. It would depend upon yourselves."

"Not entirely, sir. You who command the Dekhanies might persuade them to be neutral; to—to—in fact to throw themselves on the Royal clemency. And suppose I assured you personally two lakhs of rupees for the service, and through you all arrears of pay to your party, would that suffice?"

"Take it, friend," said Osman Beg. "My lord will give the amount in bills on Dehly or Guzerat, unless thou wait the issue and receive it here in cash. Thou canst not carry away the coin, and we cannot send it."

"I am content," said the eunuch, "for the service I shall render to the Emperor, whose name be honoured, to receive whatever may be given of his own gracious bounty."

"And remember," said the general, "that I have nothing to do with the results if the Dekhanies rise in mutiny. All that rests with them and you."

"I take the responsibility, my lord. I wish only for peace."

"You have forgotten me, Humeed Khan," said Osman Beg angrily, as they left the tent.

"Not so, friend," said the eunuch. "What I purpose will cause much confusion. The gallery of the counterscarp will be deserted, and thou knowest the way into the sally ports. Who will distinguish friends from enemies? Thou must do thy part, and I shall be able to aid thee. Fear not, one who desires a fair woman must needs do something to get her. More I cannot say; be ready on my signal, and join me. There will be enough of screaming women, and who will heed if one among them is carried away in a blanket? Surely thou hast some of thy old dare devils to help thee. If not, give up the girl."

"I cannot, and will not; she is my fate," returned Osman Beg, moodily; and for the time they separated.

For several days Abbas Khan had been diligent in his search for mines. Shafts had been sunk, and one was at last discovered which led directly under the palace. It was not loaded, and no one was guarding it; but the chamber was ready, and it could have been charged at any time. Abbas Khan, and some others with him, explored it; and, covered with dust and dirt as he was, he went direct to the Queen to tell her of it. "It will be destroyed," he said; "and even now the masons are at work building up the gallery with stones. But who can say, Mother, how many more there may be, or where they are? I have ordered cross cuttings to be carried on; but the ground is nearly rock, and the Moghul miners have skilfully followed a soft vein which they discovered, and have never quitted. Mother! mother! hear my last prayer to thee. Arise, and flee the place with the boy. When night falls, I will be with ye and guide ye forth."

"And leave ye all behind to perish? I cannot do it!" said the noble Queen, with a calm, serene expression on her countenance; "but if all could be saved, I should be grateful. I have thought over the subject night and day since it was broken between us, and this is my final determination. I am prepared for death if it should come, but not for flight, and, to my perception, dishonour. Go, see to the mine; trace others if it be possible, and to-morrow I will save all if I can. And," she added, with a confident smile, "I think I shall be successful. There is no dishonour in what the Lord hath put into my mind, and all our dear ones may be happy. Where is Zóra? Does she know of the mine?"

"No," he said, "and I will not tell her, since that danger is past."

"Then send her to me, Meeah; I would speak with her;" and he went out.

The Queen was alone in her private chamber, musing over what she purported to do. She would address the Prince Daniel himself, laying before him her desire to prevent the sacrifice of life, and offering him possession of the fort and all public property, on the condition that the garrison should march out with the honours of war.

Zóra entered as the Queen had reviewed all this in her mind, and her mistress could not help being struck with her unusual beauty and brightness. Her hair had escaped, and hung in massive waves about her shoulders; her cheeks were glowing, and her eyes sparkling with excitement.

"Oh, we have had such fun, mother; the children have been romping together, and I and some of the girls were as mad as any of them. I would thou hadst been there. But why art thou so grave: there is no bad news?"

"I have a grave task to do, daughter," she replied. "Get thy writing materials, and I will dictate. Thou canst be trusted; but I fear the secretaries, and what I tell thee must be secret till all know it." And Zóra wrote.

"And now read it all over to me again, child. While it was in my mind the purport seemed uncertain; but now that it is on paper, methinks it is clear enough." And when Zóra had read the paper, which was only a few short paragraphs, the Queen bade her make a fair copy.

"What should I do without thee, darling?" she said. "Now go and play with the children again; but be within call."

"Is Humeed Khan without?" asked the Queen of an attendant eunuch. "If so, tell him I wish to speak with him;" and he entered soon after, and sat down, making his usual salutation.

"And the mine hath been discovered," said the Queen, "under the very palace. Hast thou heard of it?"

"I have," he said. "It was dangerous; but Abbas Khan has already prevented mischief, and is searching for others."

"And the garrison; what said they?"

"There was some excitement at first, but it has subsided. All they cried was that they would defend the fort to the last, and you should lead them to victory, as you did when they followed the Standard of the Veil."

"Ah!" said the Queen, with a sigh, "those were different

times. Many were with me then who have since become traitors, and done the State irreparable injury. I have, I know, many faithful about me, but can I trust all?"

For an instant Humeed Khan thought that the remark was made for him, and the blood rushed to his dark face, almost causing it to glow. But the Queen continued—

"As I was musing upon this, Khan, it occurred to me to write a draft of a proposal to the Prince, to allow all here to pass free with their effects, and to give up the fort, which appears no longer tenable, to him, on behalf of his father. And we would fain have your opinion, as that of one of the most faithful of our officers, wise in counsel and brave in action. Read this draft, which no one but myself knows of, except her who wrote it fairly for me, and give thy opinion freely. I would save life if I can, and this appears to me the only course to pursue. Those who know me, even my enemies, will not charge me with any other motive."

Humeed Khan took the paper with a reverential gesture, and carefully perused it. As he read it he could hardly conceal his exultation and agitation. What it would have taken me days, nay weeks, to effect, he thought, she has done with her own hand, and of her own device. Surely now her time is come. Let her perish.

"It will be dangerous, lady," he said, with an affected calmness. "In their present temper the Dekhanies are not safe, and the last thing they think of is surrender. If they were to mutiny, who could stay them?"

But the Queen shook her head. "They know me and have trusted me, and I know them and trust them now. Believe me, when they know all, they will be satisfied I have done the best; but if——"

"I hear some voices without," he said, hurriedly, interrupting her. "Perhaps another mine has been discovered; perhaps ——, but your slave will return immediately." And he hastily quitted the room.

The Queen could hear no voices then without, and she sat thinking on what she had heard. There was danger, then, even from within; and those on whom she most relied might indeed, if excited, be her worst enemies. "If it be so," she said to herself, "I need not send this letter; but meet death here, or do as Meeah wishes me. And yet, no. Not that—not that; better death than flight!"

Suddenly a loud tumult of voices arose, and seemed to be approaching the palace by the plain in front. "It is this he heard," she said, and waited, with her heart throbbing. "They come close now."

It was Humeed Khan who had rushed out, as he left the Queen, into the great square where soldiers were exercising, and casting his turban on the ground, took up handfuls of dust, flinging it into the air, and crying, "Ye are betrayed! ye are betrayed, brothers! The Queen Chand is in treaty for the surrender of the fort! Deen, deen! She is not fit to live. Deen, deen! Follow me to her presence!" And he fired the rocket which was always ready for signals at the entrance.

There was no hesitation. At once, and with infuriated cries of "Treachery! treachery!" the mass surged into the great hall of audience with drawn swords, crying, "Where is the Queen? Cut her to pieces!"

The Queen had not moved except to rise from her seat, and she stood with her lips parted and her eyes distended with an absent fascination. How often in her life had a word from her quelled the wildest tumult—how often had her excitable people calmed down; but now? And yet for a moment the foremost were awed by the presence all had loved and venerated; but only for a moment. Humeed Khan, with a vile oath, rushed on and cut furiously at her with his sword, and others followed his example.

The noble woman fell covered with desperate wounds, but she still breathed; and Zóra, who had been at first appalled by the tumult, caught up her child in her arms, gave him to his nurse, and rushed to her beloved mistress's side. One ruffian would have struck her; but another said, "It is Abbas Khan's wife; let her be."

She raised the Queen's head and tried to give her water from the vessel which always stood at her side, but the Queen put her hand aside gently, and smiled. "This is death, my child. I hear—I hear—the angel—call," she gasped. "Lord!—I come;" and murmuring the Belief her head sank, and with a last sigh she breathed no more. The noble Queen's spirit was gone for ever.

Just then a number of other men rushed into the small apartment with their faces tied up, and in a moment Zóra found herself covered by a blanket and borne away among the crowd which was roaming through the palace, plundering all that could be found. She screamed, but what voice could be heard in that tumult? for there were thousands there, and still others swarmed into the great hall; but rescue was at hand.

Abbas Khan, when he had left the Queen, went back to the shaft of the mine; but as the workmen told him there was nothing more to be done at present but to continue the work that had been begun, he sat there encouraging the miners, and a number of his own guards, his faithful Beejapoor men, gathered about him. He heard the first shouts of the tumult, and all ran to the wall thinking there might be a sudden assault, but a man ran up, and cried, "To the palace! to the palace! The Queen is attacked!" and, led by their master, the whole body ran thither at their utmost speed. It needed but a glance to see what had taken place.

"Who did this?" cried Abbas Khan. "What vile traitor did this foul deed?"

"Humeed Khan," said a eunuch boy, who was sitting by the body of the Queen, weeping; "I saw him strike her first. And they have taken away Zóra-bee, and little Meeah is crying. Bring her back."

It hardly needed these words to urge the Khan on. Near the entrance of the audience hall he saw something covered with black being carried along, and the mass of his powerful men charging through the crowd soon came up with it. Osman Beg's covering had fallen from his face, but he did not see his cousin at first, nor till he was suddenly pulled back did he think he would be recognised; but he immediately attacked Abbas Khan with his sword. Neither spoke a word, but the ruffian had no chance of life, and lay dead at his cousin's feet almost before he had realised his presence.

"My poor darling," said the Khan, as he released Zóra from her bonds, "this is no place for thee. Go to Meeah. But thou art safe—blessed be Alla, thou art safe!" Truly it was no place for her. The floor around was a pool of blood, and the bodies of some strangers, among whom were several negro slaves, lay there in ghastly death with their master. Zóra cast one shuddering glance on the horrible group, and, covering her face, hurried back to her child, trembling and terror-stricken.

Meanwhile Yasin, with another body of the guard, had found Humeed Khan hiding in an ante-room, and brought him, with his arms tied together at his back, to the spot where Abbas Khan stood. "He did it! he did it!" cried a thousand voices. "Let him die!"

"Thou art not worthy of a soldier's death," said Abbas Khan, "but of a felon's. Yet, if thou wilt, say why thou didst this foul crime? What had she done to thee, who was thy benefactress for years?"

"It matters not why I did it," was the sullen reply. "I did it, and rid the world of one who had vexed it too long;" and he spoke no more. Then some men, taking him up, put a noose round his neck, and, throwing the end of the rope over the branch of a tree, left him to wrestle out his life in the air.

By this time the rest of the Abyssinians, the Arabs, and other foreigners, had assembled in the square, and the majority of the Dekhanies, who were deploring the Queen's murder with passionate weeping, separated quietly, crying to Abbas Khan to lead them against the Moghuls, for they were true to their King, of whom he was now the only protector.

## CHAPTER IX.

### CONCLUSION.

By the time Abbas Khan could reach the room to which the body of the murdered Queen had been taken, it had been laid out with the usual formalities. He could have done nothing there, and it was necessary for him to satisfy himself that no deep-laid treachery or disaffection was at work. And of these there appeared no traces. All the leaders of Dekhany parties came forward and made their salutations, as usual, and the men crowded round him with professions of attachment and devotion, which left no cause for doubt that the dreadful act that had been committed was one of sudden frenzy, enacted by the eunuch, whom he had long suspected, though undefinably, of sinister designs. He was a man in whom the Queen had reposed as great confidence as in himself; and to breathe idle suspicion to her would have been only to excite suspicion of himself, and he had not attempted to do so; but since the flight of Nihung Khan, the eunuch's manner had been changed, and the former unreserved confidence that had existed no longer continued at heart, though outwardly the two men were apparently as cordial as ever.

Satisfied that all was tranquil, and that the fort and garrison had subsided into their usual calm, Abbas Khan returned to the palace, and reverently visited the remains of his beloved mistress and mother, for he had always looked on her in the place of one; and as such, and his Queen, paid her reverence. Outside, in the hall of audience, and in the ante-chamber of the room in which she lay, were Moollas, reading and chanting the stated portions of the Koran. Incense was burning, and its smoke hung about the clustered pillars, niches, and fretted ceilings; and within, the women and eunuchs of the household were wailing, moaning, and occasionally breaking into passionate cries and adjurations. Zóra and the young mother of the boy King were sitting at the head of the Queen, with their faces covered, and heads bowed down, wailing like the rest; and as Zóra looked up, her husband saw her face and eyes swollen with weeping, and full of unutterable woe. She could not speak, and longed to throw herself into his arms. But that was not the place for such an action, and she remained kneeling.

Nor could Abbas Khan say more than the usual salutation to the dead. "Peace be with thee, and the blessing of the Lord," and burst into an almost uncontrollable passion of weeping. All the majesty, all the heroism, all the benevolence, all the political ability of the noble woman lying there, in the last sleep of death, surged up to his memory, mingled with tender thoughts of her loving kindness, her bearing with all his waywardness from boyhood; and now a traitor's sword had closed that noble life, without a warning or a suspicion.

The Queen's face was not changed, except to wear the expression of a glorious death. A soft smile, as if of peace in the last supreme moment, lingered on her lips; and though her poor slight body was covered with wounds, the face had escaped mutilation, and had become more beautiful, if possible, in death than in life. Who could forget it? and long they gazed and watched. Who ever would forget it? Zóra would fain have had him stay, for she needed comfort; but with a few soothing words he said, "I must not sleep to night, darling; but watch, too, over ye all, as is my duty. It may be that the enemy may be unquiet, and the people need all my vigilance." Then he took up his boy and kissed him, and blessed them both.

At the earliest dawn he was with the mourners again, and what remained of the Noble Queen was reverently taken up and carried to a little private cemetery in an angle of the fort, and there laid in the earth. Abbas Khan had sent a flag of truce to the Moghul trenches to say that unshotted guns would be fired for the Queen; and the salvoes of artillery which mingled with the chants of the Moollas and the wailings of the people, who crowded every point from which the last procession could be seen, were not noticed: while during the day a letter of condolence, in the name of the young King, was sent by the Prince Daniel, an act of unexpected courtesy.

We cannot linger on the sadness that fell over all. Under such circumstances a public calamity has greater effect than at any other; and sadly were the noble lady's cheering smile and hearty words of encouragement missed by all to whom they had become familiar. What was Abbas Khan to do? Who was to undertake the Regency on behalf of the young King? Zóra entreated her husband not to do so. Then, too, Ahmednugger was severed, and she longed for a peaceful existence at Beejapoor. Her life had been one of continual alarm, danger, treachery, and war, and still danger most imminent surrounded them; and yet she could not counsel flight.

The suspense was not of long duration, and after consultation with the officers of the fort, it had been determined to send a flag of truce into the Royal camp—not to write—to ascertain what terms would be given for the surrender of the fort, and the conveyance of the young King to Joonair. But the proposal was never made. Encouraged by the death of the Queen, and convinced that the garrison had lost heart, Khan Khanan redoubled his exertions, and though the great mine was disabled, yet those in the counterscarp and under the ramparts, five in all, were ready, and were loaded during that day and the next.

On the day following, masses of the Moghul troops were seen

from the cavalier to be marching upon the fort, and taking up new positions during the morning. It seemed as though new ground was to be broken to the east and north ; or a feint made to cover some operation outside. A few shots were fired at them, but they were too distant to have any effect. The movement was, however, a feint, and a successful one, for under cover of it the enemy had lodged a heavy mass of infantry as a storming party in the trenches, and soon after midday, at the hottest period, the mines in the counterscarp and rampart were fired simultaneously ; and the effect was so sudden and so unlooked for, that the enemy made his way into the ditch and up the breach, now a wide and easy one, without much loss and without check, and a scene of massacre ensued which we have no need to describe.

Abbas Khan had been sitting on the rampart, watching with several of his men, when the mine nearest them was sprung, hurling the guard of one of the smaller bastions into the air, when he felt himself struck with a large piece of stone, and remembered no more. Some of his men took him up at once, and led by the faithful Yasin, carried him to his apartments in the palace, and laid him down. But he still breathed, and Zóra, who knelt by him, could see no blood ; and through the terror of assault, and the shouts and shrieks of the combat at the breach, she continued to bathe his face and hands with water, and to rouse him to consciousness. But nearer and nearer grew the tumult, spreading on all sides; and, expecting momentary death, she knelt with her boy beside his father's body and said the last prayers of the dying. While she was thus employed a Rajpoot officer of rank, accompanied by a crowd of men, rushed in pell-mell with uplifted swords, but their commander restrained them; and Zóra, seeing his action, fell at his feet, beseeching her husband's life.

"My name is Bénee Singh," he said, "and I have led the assault. To me and my Rajpoots is committed the charge of all the treasure of the fort and the command of the palace, and we have orders to spare those we find and to protect the young King. Direct us to him, and I will leave some men to guard you and yours. Do not fear, you are safe; and we bear no enmity to wounded and helpless men. See to him, Hurpul Singh," he continued to a sub-officer; "let him not be disturbed, or the lady; and keep people out—perhaps he is dying."

But Abbas Khan was not dying. He had only been struck senseless by the blow of the stone; and after a while, to the infinite joy and thankfulness of his wife, he opened his eyes, and would have stretched out his arms to her, but one—his left—was powerless.

"What has happened, Zóra?" he said. "Why am I here? and who are these men?"

"Be still," she said, gently. "Thou art safe, and the child is safe; but the fort is taken by the mines. Dost thou not hear the tumult without?"

"And I was not with them to strike a blow in our defence! O cruel fate!" And he tried to raise his arm again, but it fell back.

"Be content, my lord," said the man called Hurpul. "It was your luck the first time, it is ours now; and we have won. Even now the gates are wide open, and masses of men are entering. Presently the Prince and Khan Khanan will come, and a salute will be fired. But is thy arm broken? Let me see. No," he continued, "it is sound, but the bruise is a bad one; and thou art as helpless as a child. Thank God for thy life as thy lady doth. Get her to make a fomentation of meem leaves and turmeric and thou wilt be relieved. When the Khan Khanan comes I will bring him hither."

Zóra hid herself when the great general came in soon afterwards, and spoke kindly to her husband. "I have not forgotten thee, Abbas Khan. From the time the treaty was executed I have wished thou wert among us, as friends of Beejapoor, rather than these faithless, fickle murderers; and thou might be so yet. Thou hast held the command here?"

"Yes, my lord," returned the Khan, "since Nihung Khan, the Abyssinian, fled. After his defeat by you I have had to do my duty."

"Well, I cannot stay, sir, now, but will come to you hereafter. I have ordered apartments for you and your household in the palace, close to the city, where you will be removed this evening, and promise that all your private property shall be sent after you. The eunuchs will, no doubt, know what it is."

That evening, in closed palanquins, Abbas Khan and his wife, the boy King and his mother, were removed to the convenient and elegant structure we have mentioned, which has been converted now into an English residence. The cool, pure, untainted air, and the pleasant shady garden, soon effected Abbas Khan's recovery from the dangerous and painful contusions he had received, and all he now desired and besought from the Prince and his general, who came frequently to converse with him, was permission to depart with his effects to Beejapoor. Both the Prince and Khan Khanan had been greatly struck by his ability and intelligence, and would fain have had him enter the Moghul army, and assume a high command, but he respectfully declined the honour. His estates in Beejapoor, with Zóra's, were very considerable. The Queen had much enriched him, and all the contents of his private treasury in the fort had been scrupulously made over to him. He had afforded all the information possible as regarded the State affairs, and he and Zóra had visited the humble grave of their beloved mistress to perform some necessary ceremonies there; but Zóra could never enter the palace; from her mind the visions of blood and slaughter it brought back would require many years to efface.

So, when a suitable opportunity offered, Abbas Khan and his family, accompanied by all his retainers who had escaped the siege, set out for Beejapoor, travelling by the route by which they had come, past Nuldroog and Almella, where they were welcomed with joy. We may imagine, too, with what hearty rejoicing his uncle and the Lady Fatima welcomed their long absent ones, and with what profuse entertainments the little Meeah, now a sturdy little fellow, was inducted into the general heirship of the house. But Abbas Khan's most impressive reception was from his King, who, grateful for his devotion to Queen Chand, received him in a grand durbar, and raised him to the highest rank of nobility, and conferred upon him other substantial proofs of his gratitude. Not long afterwards, Dilawar Khan, Viceroy of Moodgul, whose health had failed, gave up his viceroyalty and military command, and, to his wife's infinite delight, Abbas Khan accepted both with gratitude.

Before Abbas Khan had been allowed to leave Ahmednugger, the boy King, Bahadur Nizam Shah, with his mother and other female relatives, had been taken away as prisoners, and were confined in the fortress of Gwalior. All the treasures and regalia of the kingdom were confiscated and removed thither with him. Thenceforth the greatest portion of the kingdom was annexed to the Moghul empire; but for some years after, the remainder, up to the frontiers of Golconda and Beejapoor, was ruled over by Mullek Umber, on behalf of a descendant of the Royal family, who was crowned under the title of Moortuza Nizam Shah, but the family finally became extinct about the year 1607.

The Bishop and Maria were miserable until they heard the real facts of the capture of Ahmednugger. The Queen's murder had been repeated with endless exaggeration, and Abbas Khan was said to have perished with her, or in the last assault; while of Zóra nothing was known, but it was believed she had been carried away into captivity. Still they had hope, and Mullek Umber bid them hope, and despatched a trusty messenger to the city, who soon found out Abbas Khan and his wife, and brought letters from them. "We are safe," Zóra wrote to Maria, "and are going to Beejapoor. You must come too, and live together again." But the country was hardly safe yet for travelling, and they were detained till Mullek Umber could send them to Nuldroog by the way they had come. At Beejapoor they found that Abbas Khan and Zóra were already established at Moodgul, and after a short stay at the capital, they proceeded to their destination. The Bishop had applied to the King for a letter to Goa, in relation to the wealth of Dom Diego, and it was satisfactory to the worthy man that the affair had been arranged by the banker, and that the Church was the richer by several lakhs of rupees.

How thankful and how happy they all were. Nor was it long before Maria and Zóra revisited the scene of their first meeting. The old house was cleaned out for them and purified, and their first excursion from Moodgul was to that well-remembered place. Even the Lady Keysama was not above meeting the Lady Zóra Khanum, and they talked over bygone events with interest. As to Runga Naik and Burma, they were beside themselves with joy; insisting that the ladies should see the cataract from the palace at the top of the fort; that Zóra should revisit the fearful scene of her abduction and escape; and she pointed out, with eyes swimming in tears, where she had been confined, and how delivered. "Your slave only regretted that he did not go in and slay that vile ruffian in his sleep," said Burma Naik; "but the Lord reserved him for your hand, Meeah, and we rejoice that he died at your feet like a dog." This, however, was a subject which the Khan rarely alluded to, and the Beydur saw that it had better be avoided.

They revisited the place many a time afterwards, but on the first day, neither too full to be frightful, or too empty to be meagre, the noble cataract was in its full beauty; and they descended from the palace by the small path by which Zóra had been carried by Jooma, the slave, and sat down on the gun in the bastion, as they had done before. In the distance the giant fall sparkled with rainbows, and the spray at times was full of golden light, which, from the evening sun, spread itself over the rugged sides of the ravine, over the feathery foliage which clothed the crags, and the plashing water which fretted against the rocks at their feet far below. While the little Meeah, in his father's arms, pulled handfuls of flowers from the creepers which hung everywhere around, Zóra and Maria sat hand in hand without speaking; and perhaps their hearts were too full for aught else than loving and reverent memories of the past. Nor was the place ever left unvisited by Zóra in after days, when the little mosque was repaired, and prayers were said by an old Syud whom she placed in it; and she came there with her children on the sacred anniversaries of her grandfather's death. But he is forgotten now; and of the "Peer," who receives a traditional anniversary worship to this day, no name has been preserved. We may be sure that on these anniversaries no more delightful subjects for stories for the children arose, than their mother's accounts of her early perils and escapes. Once little Meeah said, looking earnestly in her face, "Mother, how didst thou escape from all these troubles?" And Zóra answered, gently, "I trusted in the Lord, my child."

Reader, who hast followed us in the course of this old world tale, we need hardly tell you that all are forgotten now; and there are traces of none except the two Beydurs, whose descendants still inhabit Korikul and Kukeyra, and are unchanged from what they used to be in the times of which I have written. For the rest, Beejapoor is a magnificent ruin, but Ahmednugger flourishes as an English station and cantonment, and the stout old fort is in perfect preservation. In both, and in the country round, nay, in all Dekhan, the memory of Chand Beebee, who defended the fort, and was murdered by her ungrateful people, and her heroic deeds and devotion in the battle of the "Standard of the Veil," are still sung and recited as the fittest memorials of

"A NOBLE QUEEN."

## NOTE.

There are no records traceable at Moodgul of the worthy Bishop and his devoted sister, but they are believed to have remained there some years, and to have eventually returned to Portugal. But the small Christian Churches so strangely preserved under the continuous Mussulman Governments of the Dekhan still survive, and are steadfast to their faith. They are still as they existed at the period of this tale—Moodgul and Raichore, with their dependencies, Chittapoor on the Bheema, and Aurungabad, and they are ministered to by priests under the jurisdiction of the Archbishop of Goa.

# GLOSSARY.

Adalut, *Court of justice.*
Ajaib! *Wonderful!*
Ajuba! *Extraordinary!*
Akhbar, *News letter.*
Alla dilaya te leonga! *If God give, I will take!*
"Alla hu Akhbar!" "*God is victorious!*"
Amán! *Mercy!*
Ameen, ameen! *Amen, amen!*
Astagh-fur-oolla! *God forbid!*
Azán, *Evening prayer.*

Bairagees, *Hindoo mendicants.*
Beebee, *Lady.*
Beydur, *Tribe of aborigines.*
Bhylmees, *Tribe of Mussulmans.*
Birianees, *A kind of Pilao.*
Bismilla! *In the name of God!*
Burkhat, Durbar Burkhat, "*The Durbar is dismissed.*"

Chabootra, *Earthen platform used for assemblies.*
Chaoree, *Village place of assembly.*
Chaya Mata, *The nymph of the fall.*
Chistee, *The designation of a tribe of Fakeers.*
Chitnees, *Correspondence clerk.*
Corus, *Anniversary.*
Cucheri, *Office for public business.*

Daad! daad! *Complaint! complaint!*
Dacoits, *Gang robbers.*
Dall, *Split pulse.*
Darogah, *Superintendent.*
Deen-deen! *For the faith! for the faith!*
Dohai! *Cry for justice.*
Doputta, *Scarf.*
Duffadar, *Inferior officer.*
Duftur, *Record Office.*
Durbar, *Court.*
Durora, *Gang robbery.*
Fatehas, *Thank-offerings.*
Feringhi, *European.*
Furashes, *Sweepers and tent pitchers.*
Futteh Mydan, *The Plain of Victory.*
Futteh-i-Nubber, *Victory to the Prophet.*

Geesoo Duraz, "*Long Locks*"—title of saint at Kulburgab.
Ghee, *Boiled butter.*
Gopal swami, *Appellation of the god Krishna.*
Goruk Imlee, *Adansonia.*
Gosha, *Privacy.*

Hai-hai! *Alas, alas!*
Hakeem, *Physician.*
Harem, *Women's apartments.*
Hari Ból, *Hindoo war-cry.*
Hoons, *A gold coin.*
Howdahs, *Seat on elephant.*
Humeenas, *Thin bag of leather worn at the waist.*
Huzrut, *Prince.*

Imáms, *Religious officers.*
Inshalla! *Please God.*

Jamahs, *Loose trousers.*
Jemadár, *Native officer.*
Jerreeds, *A game played on horseback with javelins.*
Jey mata! *Victory to the Mother!*
Julaybees, *Kind of sweetmeat.*

Kabob, *Meat roasted.*
Karámat, *Miracle.*
Kazee, *Mohamedan law officer.*
Khan, *Title of respect.*
Khanum, *Wife of Khan.*
Khedive, *Head of sect of Mussulmans.*
Khoda Hafiz, *God protect you!*
Kibleh, *Point of attraction.*
Kicheri, *Dish of rice and pulse.*
Killadar, *Governor of fort.*
Kooroo Kshetra, *The great battle between the solar and lunar races, described in Mahabarut.*
Kotwal, *Town magistrate.*
Kullunders, *Tribe of Fakeers.*

Kumkhob, *Cloth of Gold.*
Kurnum, *Village accountant.*
Kussal, *Butcher.*

Lakh, *A hundred thousand.*
Loongee, *Man's waist cloth.*
Luddoos, *Kind of sweetmeat.*

Mahabarut, *Sacred epic of the Hindoos.*
Máma, *Confidential female attendant.*
Mawallees, *A Mahratta tribe.*
Masháek, *Religious devotee.*
Mashal'a! *Praise to God!*
Meeah, *Familiar title of eldest son among Mussulmans.*
Mirdha, *Court usher.*
Mohurrum, *Mahomedan festival.*
Mohurs, *gold coin.*
Momins, *Weavers.*
Monsoon, *Rainy season.*
Moolla, *Religious teacher.*
Moonshee, *Secretary.*
"Moonskir and Nakar," *The Angels of death.*
Moorsheed, *A disciple.*
Muezzin, *Caller to prayer.*
Mufti, *Law officer.*
Mundan-ool-Ghyb, *Spirit supposed to protect travellers.*
Mynas, *Starlings.*

Nagáras, *Large kettledrums.*
Naik, *Head of Beydur tribe.*
Nalkee, *Sedan chair.*
Nawab, *Lord.*
Neem, "*Melia ardizarachta.*"
Nika, *Marriage of the second order.*
Nobut, *Band of music attached to persons of high rank.*
Nuzzur, *Offering.*

Owleas, *A saint.*

Palkee, *Litter.*
Pán, *Betel leaf.*
Patell, *Head officer of village.*
Peer, *Saint.*
Peer-i-Dustugeer, *Respectful address to a saint.*
Peshkar, *Minister of Finance.*
Pice, *Copper coin.*
Pilao, *Savoury dish of meat and rice.*
Pooja, *Hindoo worship.*
Puleeta, *A lamp charm.*
Punah, *Protection.*
Putwari, *Village accountant.*

Rámáyan, *Hindoo epic poem.*
Ranee, *Hindoo princess.*
Roostum, *One of the heroes of the Shah Nama.*
Rujub-ool-Ghyb, *A spirit supposed to watch over travellers.*
Rumzan, *Mussulman fast.*

Salaam aliekoom! *Salutation of peace.*
Sari, *Woman's garment.*
Séndhee, *Fermented palm juice.*
Shabash! *Well done!*
Shah, *King.*
Shookr, shookr! *Thanks, thanks!*
Shoolka, *Scones.*
Shubgusht, *A marriage procession by night.*
Shytan, *The Devil.*
Siah Chuttree, *Tribe of Mussulmans* —called "black umbrellas."
Soosi, *kind of cotton cloth.*
Synd, *A division of Mussulmans.*
Syndanee, *Female Synd.*
Swami, *Title of Hindoo religious princes.*

Touba! touba! *Shame! shame!*
Tukeea, *Abode of a Fakeer.*
Turreequt, *Path to salvation.*

Ul-humd-ul-illa! *Praise be to God!*
Unjeel, *The New Testament.*

Vakeels, *Agents.*

Wallee, *Saint.*

Ya, Alla, Kureem! *O Lord, most merciful.*
Ya Kureem! *O merciful!*

Zemindars, *Land owners.*
Zenana, *Women's private apartments.*
Zeels, *Portions of the Koran.*

THE END.